PERSEVERANCE OVER PAIN

A SURVIVOR'S STORY

PERSEVERANCE OVER PAIN

PAIN

A SURVIVOR'S STORY

F. LENNON

DISCLAIMER

This is a memoir reflecting the author's present recollections of experiences over time. Some names and characteristics have been changed, and some dialogue has been recreated.

May Your Soul Rest in Peace, Dad.
I Love You and I Forgive You.
Until We Meet Again.

CONTENTS

DISTINCTIVE MEMORY 1

FAMILY ORIGINS (1979-1983)... 2

TROUBLE IN PARADISE (1984-1989) 4

PRIVATE EYE (1987-1989).. 9

CONSEQUENCES (1989)..12

NEW BEGINNINGS (1990) 13

JEEPERS CREEPERS (1990)...15

SHATTERED BY TRAUMA (1991)..17

SAFETY NET (1991)..19

ON OUR OWN (1991)..25

NIGHTMARE IN MIAMI (1992) 31

HURRICANE SEASON (1992)..35

DISTRACTION (1993/1994)...38

MORE COMPLICATIONS ALONG THE WAY (1993-1994) 40

NEW MINDSET (1994-1995) 44

THE LOTTERY TICKET (1994-1995) 46

SERPENT AT THE TURF MOTEL 49

SUICIDE MISSION (1994-1995) 52

FROM FOE TO FRIEND (1994) 54

DEATH OF A LOVED ONE! (1995)...55

DREAM TEAM! (1995) 56

FED UP & FIGHTING BACK (1995)..58

SAVED (1995) 62

HIGH SCHOOL JOURNEY (1996)..73

CHURCH (1996) 78

RECONCILIATION (1997) 80

SOCIAL LIFE AT SCHOOL (1997).................................. 83

LIFE OUTSIDE OF SCHOOL (1996-1997) 86

UNKNOWN ABILITY (1997)... 91

BASKETBALL JUNKIE! (1998)....................................... 105

SHOW AND PROVE (1998-1999) 107

SOMEONE INTRIGUING (1998) 112

SUMMER LEAGUE DEBACLE (1999) 114

ABRUPT CHANGES (1999) 117

GUESS WHOSE BACK (2000) 119

SENIOR PRANK (2000) 126

UNPLEASANT SURPRISE (MAY 2000)......................... 130

GRADUATION PRESENT (2000) 132

DEATH OF A FORMER TEAMMATE (2000)................. 136

ALMOST LOST IT ALL (2000) 138

OFF TO COLLEGE (2000) 141

LOVE INTEREST BACK HOME (2000)......................... 144

SUMMER WORK (2001) 147

CAR HUNTING (2001) 150

THE ACCIDENT (2001).. 152

NEW LIVING ARRANGEMENTS (2001) 154

UNEXPECTED COMPANION (2001)............................. 156

LOSS OF A LOVED ONE (2001) 158

CREATIVE OUTLET (2002).. 160

MORE DEVASTATING NEWS (2002)............................ 163

THE RETURN (JUNE 2002) 165

RIP GREAT-GRANDMA (2002) 167

WILD GOOSE CHASE (2002)...169

JUNIOR YEAR AT FAU (AUG 2002)...171

DOUBLE VISION (SEPT 2002)..173

FINALLY, IN THE STUDIO (OCT 2002) 176

THE MAIN THING (2002)...181

CHRISTMAS BREAK (2002) 183

ANOTHER ACCIDENT (2002) 185

THE DEVIL'S LETTUCE (2003)...190

THE END (FEB 2003) 194

SENIOR YEAR (2003-2004)...196

NEW LIVING ARRANGEMENTS (2004) 199

A PRIZED POSSESSION (JUNE 2004)..201

GRADUATION (AUG 2004) 203

PROBATION OFFICER (2004-2007) 204

SOMETHING NEW (2004)...208

FAMILY HELPING FAMILY (2005) 210

ATTEMPTED ABDUCTION (2005) 212

UNEXPECTED LOSS (SEPTEMBER 11, 2006)...214

TURNING OF THE TIDE (2007)..215

MOVING ON (2007) 218

MY NEW CAREER (AUG 2007)..222

STRATEGIC MOVES (2007)...225

CHURCH IN THE RAW (2007)...229

EMERGENCY CALL (2007) 230

ASSISTANT COACHING (2007) 232

UNEXPECTED DEATH (2008) 235

RECOGNITION (2008) 237

MY SECOND YEAR (2008-2009) 239

INGRATIATED IN THE WORD (2009) 242

ANOTHER CHAMPIONSHIP (2010-2011) 246

SOMETHING NEW (2011-2012) 248

GETTING THINGS SITUATED (2012) 253

WEDDING DAY (JUN 2012) 254

A BLESSING FROM GOD (JUL 2012) 255

COMPLICATIONS (JAN 2013) 258

SURPRISES (2013) 260

FAMILY FALLOUT (2013) 263

THE SEASON (JAN-MAR 2013) 265

ABRUPT END TO COACHING (2014) 266

MY DAD GOES MISSING (2014) 269

UNEXPECTED REQUEST (DEC 2013) 270

WELL-ROUNDED (2016) 274

TRAVEL BALL EXPERIMENT (2016) 276

SACRIFICES (2017) 280

DAD'S HEALTH (2017) 282

A NEW ENVIRONMENT (2017-2018) 283

SEARCHING FOR A TEAM (2018) 285

NEW EXPERIENCES (2018-2019) 287

HUMBLING EXPERIENCE (APR 2019) 292

NEAR FATAL ACCIDENT (2019) 295

NEW SEASON, NEW HOPE (2019-2020) 297

RECOGNITION (2020) 303

POTENTIAL FOR GROWTH (2021) 304

GRANNY (MARCH 2022)...307

ENJOYING NETTA'S JOURNEY (2020-2024)..308

REST IN PEACE (2024) 310

Distinctive Memory

I can recall the life-changing moment as if it were yesterday. It's a vivid memory that still haunts me whenever it crosses my mind.

At the time, I was a clueless and innocent ten-year-old, sitting in an empty stairwell, contemplating why my father had us there. It was approximately twelve o'clock on a rainy Saturday night. Wet, filthy, and pitch black would perfectly describe the area that surrounded us. The main thing I could see at the moment was the flame from my dad's lighter as he put it up to his "makeshift" crack pipe. He created it with the silver foil from the inside of an empty Newport cigarette carton. The more he insisted I turn away from him and look elsewhere, the more my curiosity got the best of me. I attempted to act as if I wasn't paying attention to what he was doing by playing with the tiny, dime-sized hole in the bottom of one of my sneakers, but I was drawn to my father's current illegal activity like a moth to a flame. At the moment, I was oblivious to the fact that our lives had already begun to spiral out of control.

This would be the first, but certainly not the last time, witnessing the man I viewed as my provider and protector "transform" into someone whom I could no longer recognize with each hit of crack cocaine he indulged in. Nothing could prepare me for the struggle and adversity I would face from that point on.

1

Family Origins (1979-1983)

To shed light on how everything began, I will start with my parents. Their relationship started like something one would see at the beginning of a typical Tyler Perry movie. Then it escalated into a relationship you would see in a daytime soap opera like "The Young and The Restless" or "As the World Turns."

My mother grew up in a household with a bunch of brothers (which contributed majorly to the development of her assertive personality). She is the "no-nonsense" type that'll address any sign of disrespect swiftly, verbally, and physically, if need be.

My father, however, grew up in a household with more than a few siblings. From all accounts, he was stubborn, witty, very athletic, a certified ladies' man, and confrontational, just like my mother.

My parents met each other while they were both in the military. My mother was nineteen years young and in Advanced Individual Training for the Army Reserves, while my father was twenty years old and in Advanced Individual Training for the Army Infantry. The two of them were inseparable from the beginning. No more than a year later, they were married in a small military-inspired ceremony.

Just about the entire family was happy for him—everyone except for my grandmother, unfortunately. According to my father, his mother was irate about the marriage because soon afterward, he would stop sending money home for her to "put up" for him. Once he got married, he decided to put his money in a personal bank account, since he now had a family of his own to take care of. My grandmother allegedly claimed my mom was the reason her son stopped sending her money, as if the money was wired to her for her own personal use.

Bo was one of the two unique nicknames my dad was given while growing up in the Coconut Grove and Opa Locka communities of Miami, Florida. About a year and a half after their wedding, my mother got pregnant with me. During that time, my father was stationed in Columbus, Georgia, which is where I was born (1982). There were a few complications with my birth, and my mother was forced to have an emergency C-section.

I was born prematurely and only weighed a few pounds. According to my medical records, I spent a few weeks in the hospital before my parents were finally able to take me home. Seemingly, they didn't waste any time because soon after giving birth to me, they conceived my sister. She was born while our family was relocated to Honolulu, Hawaii, by the military, where my father was stationed for a brief time (1983). All seemed fine with my parents during this time, but behind the scenes, more was going on than anyone realized.

Trouble in Paradise (1984-1989)

Not long after my sister was born, we constantly traveled throughout the United States until we finally landed in Huntsville, Alabama. This was where the most troublesome issues began between my parents. Huntsville, Alabama, would be the destination where we resided for an extended period. To be exact, we lived on and around the Redstone Arsenal military base for approximately five years (1984-1989). We would find ourselves relocating to various locations throughout Huntsville for some strange reason.

Living on and around the military base seemed like a utopia of sorts. My sister and I spent many joyful days, when we were not attending school at Ridgecrest Elementary, riding our bikes by ourselves through the numerous riding paths and playing with our friends, Starla and Brian.

We were so carefree and completely oblivious to the potential dangers of the great outdoors. It seemed as if our parents had eyes and ears everywhere, especially since we were left unattended so much. Some of my fondest memories from that time include venturing into the desolate woods, catching fireflies with mason jars, and storing them on our bedroom windowsill

. Unquestionably, I guess you could say my sister and I had a typical sibling relationship. We loved hanging around one another most of the time, but there were days when we couldn't stand to be around each other. To be perfectly honest, since I was the oldest, I felt she should do whatever I told her to do, whenever I told her to do it. My sister, on the other hand, wasn't a pushover by any means. She was a fighter like our mom and dad. I was usually the one who shied away from any potential verbal and/or physical confrontation. That never deterred me from doing vindictive things to bother her, though, such as removing the arms of her Barbie dolls and popping their heads off just before I'd toss them under our bunk bed at night. I clearly had some underlying anger issues I needed to work out.

Consequently, our parents would force us to hug and reconcile afterward to help us resolve any personal issues. We were too young and immature to understand it back then, but now I can appreciate their efforts in attempting to teach us to love one another beyond our various disagreements.

Regardless of the lessons they tried to teach us, our parents were not without their faults. For instance, I can recall one specific night when I was thirsty and I got out of the top bunk of our bunk bed to go to the kitchen. I remember seeing a manila envelope on the kitchen table with what I figured was dirt or tiny pieces of crumbled leaves lined up outside of it. I would have never imagined the mysterious substance my parents had on the table was actually marijuana. To this day, I still don't know if they were preparing to smoke or sell it, even though my mother denied having anything to do with the substance I saw.

Regardless, I recall there was an abundance of incense burning back in the day. I guess they thought they were slick by trying to mask the smell of the weed in our apartment. The most frequent incident I recall from back then was the constant domestic violence that took place in our household.

One particular Friday night, I vaguely remember my father and mother having a heated argument, which escalated when he shoved her into the living room wall after she said something he didn't like. Upon her being shoved, she sprinted to the kitchen quicker than a bolt of lightning and grabbed a huge butcher's knife. Prior to that incident occurring, I never remembered seeing that monstrosity of a knife before. As a little boy, it was the biggest knife I'd ever seen (The type of butcher knife Jason Voorhees used in the Friday the 13th movies). My sister and I were beyond scared, and to use the word "terrified" would be an understatement. Afterward, our mom hysterically ran after our father until he sprinted out of the apartment.

Shortly afterward, my father returned with a couple of men in army fatigues, the letters M.P. (Military Police) affixed to their sleeves. They told him he would have to find somewhere else to lay his head for the night until things cooled down. He was allowed to grab a few articles of clothing, some toiletries, and his wallet while his military escorts were there. I think he may have stayed somewhere on the army base that night because when he eventually came back, he was wearing his army uniform.

After the dreadful but somewhat comical domestic violence that took place between our parents, they eventually reconciled, and everything seemingly returned to normal.

**

Near-Death Experience

On a Saturday, during one of the warmer summer days, we all went to the local swimming pool. My sister and I were excited because, before we went, we had only seen people swimming in movies and on television. When we arrived at the community pool, I noticed older kids were jumping off a diving board. I became intrigued immediately. I'd never seen a diving board in person before. Not only that, but I was captivated by the notion of possibly putting my feet on it and jumping until I couldn't jump anymore. Despite being young and small in stature, I still wanted to have a great time and do the things the older kids were doing. There was only one minor issue I didn't consider: I didn't know how to swim.

As we put our things down in the area our parents had chosen, our mother advised me to keep an eye on my sister while we were near the kiddie pool area and not to wander off while they were "getting things situated." So, we remained near the kiddie pool until they returned. I held my sister as she continued to squirm and push my hands away. She was desperately trying to get me off her so she could get a closer look at the pool water, but I refused to let her go until one of our parents returned. From afar, I saw our father talking to a random guy near the male and female restrooms. Conveniently, he ran into one of his army buddies, and they were conversing for a long time about the upcoming military football game they were playing in soon. Our mother returned and was tending to my sister near the kiddie pool. As for me, I had my sights set on the diving board the older kids were on when we first arrived.

As I inched closer to the diving board, I kept a steady eye on where my parents were, to see if they were watching. Since they weren't, I picked up the pace a bit. I peeked over to where the lifeguard's chair was, and I also noticed they weren't there at that moment. As I made it to the diving board without being noticed, I first put my left foot on it, then worked up the courage to put my right foot on as well. I could've sworn at that time I would've been caught, but no, everyone seemed so distracted by the things they were engaged in. As I used my weight to push the diving board down with my body, I didn't realize how wet it was until I slipped

7

and fell into the deep end of the pool. I tried to scream, but every time I opened my mouth, I inadvertently inhaled abundant amounts of water.

The commotion I was making in the water was enough to get everyone's attention. I vividly recall seeing a rather heavy-set lady in a black one-piece bathing suit while I was unsuccessfully attempting to come up for air. I also remember flailing my arms and unintentionally hitting the woman until I blacked out.

When I finally came to, I was outside the pool, lying on the ground with my parents and other people scattered around me, with a look of concern on their faces. Apparently (according to my dad), the lady with the black bathing suit was in the right place at the right time. She just so happened to be in the area near where I fell in, and she was also the one who saved my life by pulling me out of the pool before I could drown.

After my dramatic rescue, it was clear that our mom and dad were both relieved and concerned at the same time. When we made it to our car, it was a different story. My mom said, "Didn't I tell you to stay near me and don't wander off? How'd you even get over there? My dad chimed in with, 'I bet his ass will listen next time, won't he! After that situation, I developed a severe fear of pools and large bodies of water.

Private Eye (1987-1989)

It's strange how some memories stay with you—etched into your mind with a clarity that time can't erase. I remember those moments from my childhood not just as events, but as feelings—confusion, curiosity, and a quiet awareness that I understood more than I let on.

My parents, like many, had their share of struggles. I knew about the occasional drinking and the tension that sometimes lingered in the air. There were other things that they tried to shield from my sister and me. At times, our mom and our dad seemed to live separate lives, even though they were legally married.

One night, I heard a strange and unfamiliar voice coming from their room. At first, I told myself it was probably just the TV, but my gut feeling told me it was something completely different.

Beforehand, I noticed that one of our parents came into our room to check to see if we were awake, and I pretended to be sound asleep, something I had gotten good at. I wasn't sure what I had overheard, but I knew it was something I wasn't meant to. After the apartment grew quiet again, the front door slowly but steadily opened and then closed. I crept to the window in our room, hoping to catch a glimpse of anything out of the ordinary, but all I saw were the fading taillights of a car disappearing into the night after pulling out of the parking lot. Someone was doing something suspicious, though I had no way of knowing who or what it was at the time.

That moment didn't come with answers, just a deeper sense that life was more complicated than I had realized. It was the first time I understood that adults, even the ones we love most, had things they unsuccessfully attempted to hide from their children.

As far as I was concerned, I knew I was one of the nosiest little boys in the world. In my adolescent mind, I thought I was reenacting scenes from the private-eye movies I used to watch with my dad. Our parents probably assumed that since my sister and I were so little, they could easily do sneaky things without us finding out. This may have been true for my sister, but not for me. I was fully aware of some of the things they were engaging in.

When my father had a chance to spend some father-son time alone with me, I would carefully plan to ask him about the other night. Every time I would get ready to ask, my plans consistently failed because our parents were fighting all the time. I ended up withholding the questions because I didn't want to potentially make the situation worse. I guess one could say I feared what he might've done if I let him know that I was aware of something that was going on that wasn't necessarily my business. He was a big proponent of "a kid staying in a kid's place," most of the time.

I remember one Saturday afternoon afterward, there was a perfect opportunity to ask him what was going on behind the scenes between him and our mom. He and I were riding in his car, headed to the corner store to purchase some Magnum Malt Liquor and cigarettes for the two of them. My dad had a two-door coupe at the time. He was blasting Easy-E's "Boyz-n-The-Hood. The lyrics were hard-hitting and bold:

"'Cause the boyz n tha hood are always hard; you come talking that trash, we'll pull your card, knowing nothing in life but to be legit. Don't quote me, boy, 'cause I ain't said s**t."

All the car windows were down, and the speakers were pounding so loudly that everyone we passed stopped and stared; some nodded their heads to the beat, while others shook their heads in disapproval. My dad let me ride in the passenger seat, like he often did, especially when my mother wasn't around. After going into the store with him to make the intended purchase, I decided to tell my dad what I knew about the other night, but unfortunately, the words wouldn't come out for some reason.

When we returned home, I immediately ran to my room and cried because I felt like a coward for "chickening out." Later that evening, while my father was watching his favorite football team, the Dallas Cowboys, play against the Miami Dolphins, he asked me why I had been in the room for so long. I tried to think of a lie to tell. After about ten seconds, I switched the subject by asking him whether the beer he was drinking was good or not, and he fell for the trick hook, line, and sinker.

He said, "Here, taste it!"

At this point, I knew I had succeeded in my goal of switching the subject, but I realized I needed to take things a step further to fully divert attention from the question my dad had asked. I followed his suggestion and took a sip of the beer he had in the cupholder of his reclining chair. As soon as the liquid touched my lips, I spat the unimaginably disgusting brew out so quickly that it looked as if it were hot lava spewing out of a volcano. It took me about thirty minutes to adequately rinse the taste out of my mouth while in the bathroom. After stalling for so long, it was now time for bed, and my deceptive goal was effectively accomplished.

Consequences (1989)

In 1989, when I was seven years old, my father was honorably discharged from the military for "Misconduct—Commission of a Serious Offense." At the time of his discharge, he was a sergeant. Apparently, he orchestrated and implemented a plan to illegally sell military equipment.

Years later, I found out he was the brains of the operation, and when someone made a substantial transaction for him, they were caught red-handed. After being interrogated, the guy who snitched on my dad implicated everyone who was involved to avoid facing the worst possible consequences. When other high-ranking officials approached my dad, he initially denied all the allegations, which resulted in him being hit with a "court-martial."

A court-martial is a military court of officers appointed by a commander to try a person or people for offenses under military law (to court-martial someone means to send a member of the armed forces for trial in a military court).

When presented with the evidence, potential sentencing, and the confession obtained by high-ranking officials from his running mate, he agreed to accept an honorable discharge rather than deny and fight the allegations. After my father's discharge from the military, we relocated to my father's hometown of Miami, Florida.

New Beginnings (1990)

It was 1990 when my family and I arrived in good old South Florida. We immediately moved into the Summer Winds Apartments in North Miami Beach.

An obvious eye-catcher in the surrounding area of the apartments was the old Coppertone sign that read, "Coppertone Welcomes You to Miami!" The message most certainly wasn't the most memorable aspect of the sign, though. In front of the message was a huge cutout of a female toddler with blonde pigtails and a dog tugging at her clothes. The crazy part about the sign was that the cutout of the dog would move up and down as if it were actually chasing the girl. The sign and its functions mesmerized me during that time.

Regarding the overall landscape, the Summer Winds complex was massive. They had multiple buildings and pools on the premises.

Our new school, Biscayne Gardens Elementary, was within walking distance of where we lived. After the first few weeks of school, my sister and I would walk there and back during the week. Since I was the oldest, our dad told me to keep a lookout while walking down the street and to ensure my sister was safe at all times. I took pride in ensuring she walked on the opposite side of the sidewalk, away from the street. When we would head to and from school, I felt more like her bodyguard than her brother. As for our parents, they couldn't pick us up from school because they had to go to work early in the morning and didn't get home until around five.

Our father used his personal and professional connections to get a job with a vending machine company near the Port of Miami. His role with the company was to help deliver and service the machines. Our mom worked at a supermarket.

Around this time, I was eight years old, and my dad convinced me to rock a god-awful rat tail in the back of my head. He claimed it was a cool thing to have at that moment.

Unfortunately, this wouldn't be enough to curb my severe self-esteem issues. For some reason, girls would shy away from having any interaction with me. Every time I looked at myself in the mirror, I felt disgusted and ashamed. I was envious of my parents' and sister's looks because everyone seemed to look nice, and I felt I looked like one of the long-lost Garbage Pail Kids. Due to my distorted vision of myself, I operated like an introvert, and my only real friend was my sister.

Jeepers Creepers (1990)

One day, as my sister and I were walking home from school, I noticed a middle-aged white male in a blue two-door Pontiac riding slowly behind us. He was trailing us conspicuously, but my dad trained me to be aware of my surroundings. I used my peripheral vision to keep track of how far he was from us. Then suddenly, the car sped past a bit and pulled over to a grassy area near the sidewalk we were on.

After we walked up a few inches, the man yelled out, "Hey, kids, come over here for a minute!"

So, like the protective older brother I considered myself to be at the time, I immediately told Grace to keep walking while I crept toward the direction of the man's car. Extreme caution was used while approaching to see what the guy wanted.

The first thing I said was, "What do you want, sir?"

When I got close to the car's passenger-side window, the man was visibly holding his penis in his hand. Shocked and confused, I quickly turned my head and raced to grab my sister's hand, and we ran all the way to our apartment complex. We were four or five minutes away from our desired destination, but we traveled as fast as our little legs could carry us. Luckily, Grace was just as fast as I was, and she shockingly almost beat me home. While running, we didn't look back in the stranger's direction. All I could hear was Grace asking me, "What's wrong?" over and over again until we made it home safely.

That ordeal was terrifying, and it could've led to something more drastic occurring, but for some strange reason, I didn't bother to mention what happened to our parents. I didn't want to bring the situation up because I felt embarrassed to do so. My sister spilled the beans about running home after school. When they asked me what happened, I broke down crying as I told them what happened. The memory of the creepy guy is one I tried to forget. It was my first lesson in the importance of being aware of my surroundings at all times.

Shattered by Trauma (1991)

In 1991, my mother suddenly decided she would leave my father and return to Alabama.

She had grown sick and tired of our father and his theatrics. It was terrible timing, considering that a few weeks before deciding to leave, our dad was laid off from his job.

The morning my mother planned to leave our father, he was completely unaware and still in the bedroom sleeping. Our mother, while moving throughout the apartment in stealth mode, got our bags packed and ready to go, without doing anything to alert our father that we were about to leave him. I remember the three of us were sitting in the living room with our suitcases and bus tickets while waiting for the taxi to arrive. As soon as our mom said we were going to leave as soon as our ride arrived, something came over me, and I ran into my parent's room to wake my dad up so I could inform him of what our mom was planning to do. When he got up, he looked like he'd seen a ghost.

His first words as he confronted our mom were, "Where the hell do you think you're going with my kids?"

A few seconds later, our mom called my dad's brother and one of his sisters over to talk some sense into our dad, because she was visibly shaken and scared of what he would do in the heat of the moment. When she finally got ready to leave, she grabbed my sister's hand forcefully and told me to come on! Once she began to walk through the threshold of the front door into the hallway, I swiftly ran to my father and bear-hugged his leg. I told my mother I was not going anywhere without "my daddy!"

17

In response, my mother looked at me with a furious look on her face and stated, "Oh well, forget it; stay here then!"

She had every right to be upset because I seemingly chose my dad over her, but the truth was, I didn't want anyone to go anywhere, even though I never effectively communicated it. When the taxi finally arrived, my mom and sister went to the Greyhound bus station, and my dad, my uncle, my aunt, and I met them there. After a few failed attempts to convince my mom to stay, my sister and my mother boarded the bus and left town.

That single moment was one of the many incidents that would impact me the most during those times. Afterward, our lives changed forever, and things went from bad to worse. We continued to live in our apartment until my dad could break the leasing agreement, about a month later.

Safety Net (1991)

Since my father was still unemployed, we had to move in with his mother to an area commonly known as "Behind Tha P" in Opa Locka. My father and his siblings were all raised there. Thankfully, Golden Glades Elementary was around the corner, and it was the school I ended up transferring to.

As for my grandmother, she had a larger-than-life personality. She was the head honcho of the entire family, and in her household, it was always her way or the highway. Don't get me wrong, Granny loved her family, but she also had no problem telling anyone and everyone what was exactly on her mind. Moving in with her was a major adjustment for my father and me, to say the least. She was the queen of predictable routines. She worked at the bus compound for the Miami-Dade County School District. She would always come home after stopping by "the number lady's house" or Phillip's Gas Station to play her daily lottery numbers.

Our first weekend at her house was a complete culture shock for me. At around 8 A.M., early Saturday morning, I would be awakened by F.C. Barnes' "Can't You See What Drugs Are Doing" blasting through the Kenwood stereo system. At the same time, a vacuum cleaner was heard rolling over the clear plastic protector runners Granny had strategically spread throughout her house. Part of me assumed she was crazy as hell for making all that noise so early in the morning; however, the other part of me started to enjoy the music. It was undoubtedly catchy at the time, and it had an old-school church choir vibe. I even recall singing the lyrics at one point:

"You need to get up off of that cocaine and get up off of that crack; you need to get yourself together and get your mind back, can't you see for yourself what drugs are doing?"

My father wasn't as enthusiastic about the song as I was, and later I would find out why. Eventually, when I got out of bed from the guest bedroom I was sharing with my dad, I said, "Good morning," to Granny, and she quickly responded with, "Good morning, Markey," instead of the actual way my middle name was supposed to be pronounced, which is "Marque."

I didn't make a big deal of it. Granny was known for taking back-talk as a sign of disrespect, and I did not feel like getting slapped during that good old Saturday morning. After we greeted each other, she told me to grab the vacuum cleaner from her and finish vacuuming while she made breakfast.

When I finished, I reached the conclusion I was done until she said, "Alright now, I need you to go dump the garbage cans from the bathrooms and take it outside; they're full!

My first thought was, "Man, I didn't even get a chance to wash my face or eat yet." But this would be a common theme for the month or two my father and I temporarily lived with her.

***

After breakfast, my dad's childhood friend Will came by and picked us up in his van to wash a few cars and earn some quick cash.

This physically imposing man was a cool and smooth dude. He kept a leather hat on his head (regardless of the weather) and a toothpick in his mouth every time I'd seen him. During this time, he was dating one of my dad's sisters, my Aunt Sable.

20

She was a phenomenal singer at Mount Tabor Baptist Church (located in Liberty City) and the fashion icon of the family. She dressed to impress everywhere she went (she got that from Granny).

Will owned his own car wash and detailing business. Per a previous conversation he had with my dad, he took it upon himself to invite him to work with him. After picking us up, we went to Consumer Meat Market in Carol City to wash a few cars. For each one we washed, Will made between twenty and thirty-five dollars per car. There was a 70/30% split on the profits. After we finished for the evening, which was around 10 P.M., instead of letting Will drop us off back at Granny's house, we went to Burger King and grabbed something to eat. I remember it like it was yesterday; back then, Whoppers were a dollar.

Once we finished eating, my dad and I walked back to Opa Locka, but we didn't go back to Granny's house just yet. We went to a stranger's house, where my father handed him the rest of the money we had left over from the cars we washed. The stranger then gave him a few small items I couldn't identify at first. Once the transaction was done, we walked all the way back to Carol City, towards the flea market. I kept asking my dad where we were going, and then he said, "We'll be headed back home shortly; come on and hurry up!" Immediately, I shut my mouth and sped up the pace of my stride. After a few minutes, we finally arrived at the stairwell that was previously described at the beginning of this story in the "Distinctive Memory" section.

The stairwell was in an old two-story building on the corner of 179th and 27th Avenue. Ironically, it was directly across the street from the Burger King where we ate earlier that night. It was my first time watching my dad make a pipe and smoke crack. It was definitely an eye-opener. I can still recall the smell and almost taste the secondhand smoke my dad attempted to blow in the opposite direction, to no avail. When he was done, he seemed to transform into someone I'd never seen before. His eyes practically bulged out of his head, and he had this odd bounce in his step.

As we walked back toward Granny's house, I tried to process what I'd seen. I thought to myself, "Maybe, just maybe, this was the reason why my mom couldn't wait to leave him." We returned home so late that I figured we'd see the sun come up. Thank God Granny and my step-grandfather were sound asleep because I know they would've had an issue with us returning so late at night.

***

Granny's house had its ups and downs. Yes, I disliked the chores and many of the things I was ordered to do, but on the other hand, I did enjoy spending time with my family. I had no idea what she meant by putting me to work was her way of "training me up." She figured if I became a jack of all trades at a young age, I would be capable of taking care of myself when I became an adult. I would hear constant stories from my dad and his siblings about the type of workload they were forced to endure growing up, so I didn't feel too bad.

During those days, I didn't really think much about my mom or my sister. In my adolescent mind, I figured they'd be right back after a while.

***

Eventually, my father began disappearing for hours at a time during the evenings, especially on weekdays. Come to find out, he was stealing things from Granny's house, taking them to the pawn shop, and selling them to people around the neighborhood. There were times I would watch him take little things to sell for drug money. Here and there, he would take me with him to make these transactions.

One day, my Grandpa Theodore received a call from a friend saying he saw my dad heading down 32nd Avenue with his lawnmower. Something told Grandpa Theodore to check the local pawn shops in the area. He was eventually able to find his lawnmower at a shop in the heart of Opa Locka. That night, when my dad came home, a huge falling out occurred between them. Grandpa Theodore and Granny were so furious that my dad was barred from the house when they weren't home. I was still fine to be there, no matter who was or wasn't home.

Sadly, I started engaging in the same behavior my dad exposed me to. For instance, I remember a girl in my class whom I liked at the time. Her birthday was approaching, and I didn't have any money, so I came up with the bright idea to go into the jewelry case located in Granny's room and take one of her custom jewelry rings to present it to my crush. After gifting her with the ring one day at school, somehow and someway, Granny came home a little late from work and called me into her room. She stuffed her hand in her pocket and pulled out the same ring I took to give to my crush at school.

She immediately asked me, "Where did you get this ring from?

I stuttered while trying to come up with the perfect lie and said, "Oh, I found it in the PE field while at school and gave it to a friend."

She looked at me like she wanted to curse or lay hands on me.

She asked me a second time, "I know you're lying; where did you get my ring from?"

23

Startled while trying to figure out another quick lie, I remained silent as if I had previously been read my Miranda rights. Granny physically and verbally tore me up that evening, and I never took anything from the house ever again.

I was so ashamed of what I did, so much so that I walked on eggshells for the remainder of the time we stayed with them. The worst part was that Granny loved talking on the phone with friends, family, church members, associates, and anyone else who enjoyed the latest gossip. I knew she was going to tell the world what I had done, and there wasn't a way to escape that harsh reality. Although I was only nine years old at the time, I truly knew my actions were wrong. Did I really feel shame in what I had done, or was the shame attributed to getting caught?

On Our Own (1991)

After the stealing incident, we finally moved out of Granny's house and into an efficiency within the same neighborhood. An efficiency is a dwelling with all the living spaces contained within one room and is less than six hundred square feet.

To take care of our basic needs and earn the money to pay the rent, my dad was still washing cars with Will. We also received food stamps and a few items, such as cheese, bread, and large cans of peanut butter (among other items).

I was still in the fourth grade, and it took me a while to get adjusted to my new school, especially once I began developing extreme focusing issues during class. Academically, it was hard for me to pay attention to the teacher during instruction, since my mind wandered all the time. All sorts of strange things and past events would randomly run across my mind.

Socially, it was a different story. I would begin to acquire a couple of associates with whom I would converse throughout the day. Having peers to talk to sort of alleviated a little of the stress I was under while trying to process all that was transpiring with me and my father. I never discussed personal matters with any of the associates I spoke with since I was raised by the old phrase, "What happens in this house, stays in this house."

Outside of school, one thing that kept me from totally losing hope was that my grandmother didn't live too far from us. I believed that if times got too rough, we could always go over to her house. During this period of time, my father and I started to really struggle and hit rock bottom.

When the rainy season began, my dad's work slowed to a crawl, and he started selling the food stamps we received from WIC for cash (WIC is a special supplemental nutrition program for Women, Infants, and Children). Back then, we received physical food stamps, unlike the debit card system they have now.

My dad and I used to take the food stamp booklets to various "Arab stores" in Opa Locka and Overtown to exchange them for cash. To paint a clear picture of how it went, let's say we had $200 worth of food stamps. We would go to any corner store throughout the numerous hoods in Miami, and my dad would tell the owner he was looking to sell some food stamps. If they expressed interest, my dad would let them know he wanted $150 cash in exchange for a book of $200 worth of stamps. At one time or another, he'd get lucky and get the asking price, and other times, he would get a little more than half.

Back in those days, food stamps were only good for buying food, and drug dealers wouldn't accept them, so my dad was highly motivated to find a suitable amount of money to go on one of his many drug binges.

The funny thing about it was that I had no idea selling food stamps was illegal until I got older. These transactions were good for temporary fixes, not for the long term.

In school, I was basically an outcast due to my poor social skills and my shabby wardrobe. Most of the clothes I owned were either in storage, sold, or lost somewhere. For the months we lived in our efficiency, we had to wash our clothes in the sink. Afterward, we'd hang them up on the clothesline located on the side of the house. It was a different experience for me since I started as a military brat. I went from getting whatever I wanted, whenever I wanted it, to having nothing. It was a humbling experience, to say the least.

The worst things got at home, the worst they got at school. Some of my classmates started following me home to pick on me and say things like, "Nando lives in a shack!" "Nando is bummy!" and so on. That sort of thing really bothered me all the time, and it led to a few altercations within those few months. Since I was smaller than my peers, they often attempted to bully me. The kids my size or smaller wouldn't bother me too much; it was always the biggest kids who couldn't resist the temptation, I guess.

***

Thankfully, I had one good friend back then by the name of Michael. Michael lived down the street from me with his grandparents. His mother and my father had previously known each other, as they had attended high school together. Now and then, when I went to Michael's grandparents' house, they would often ask me if I wanted something to eat, which was always a nice gesture. Sadly, my father and I had to move again because my dad couldn't keep up with the rent due to his expensive drug habit. At the beginning of December 1991, we moved into a house located across the street from Michael's grandparent's house. We were fortunate to rent a room there for a few months.

***

My dad started to get steady employment through the local labor pool service. A labor pool is essentially the group of people who work on an as-needed, daily basis. If you are selected to work at or for a particular job site, you'll receive a check at the end of your work shift. Sometimes my dad would have to meet construction site foremen at certain pickup spots to be provided a ride on the back of their pickup trucks. Many times, there were too many potential workers and not enough space on the trucks; therefore, transportation was on a first-come, first-served basis.

Basically, if he didn't get in the truck quickly enough, he didn't work that day. So, my dad would have to get up extremely early in the morning, to the point it was still dark outside, just to beat everyone else to the labor pool pickup site to secure a spot. In some cases, he wouldn't return home until 6 or 7 P.M., Monday through Friday.

There were many days when I was left to fend for myself. Most of the time, I made sure to get to school before the late bell, even though there were times when I overslept. Since the school breakfast was a necessity for me, I made sure not to make it a habit I indulged in often.

Academically, I was very far behind my peers in all subject areas, and I quickly discovered that having a quiet demeanor and staying low-key in class had its perks. Teachers never really bothered me much, probably because I didn't make waves in their classrooms. It was usually the students who had behavioral issues or the teacher's pets who were picked to participate. As for me, I just went through the motions and found ways to make it appear as if I was a decent student academically. Guess one could say I was just passed along—just a typical experience in the Dade County public school system.

After school, I would race home to put my bookbag in our room because I was determined to go back outside to play football with the kids who lived on our block. Devin, Marcus, and a few others, and I used to play street football until their parents yelled out their names once the streetlights came on. Once every blue moon, my father would come home, see us down the street, and throw the football around a bit. Sadly, he was usually high out of his mind while doing so, though there were some moments when he wasn't. I missed the old version of my dad a lot.

***

Santa, Where Are You?

As the Christmas season approached, all of my classmates were so excited and looking forward to spending time with their families, eating terrific soul food, and enjoying time off from school. For me personally, I came to the realization that I wasn't going to see my mom and sister ever again. A certain level of depression started to set in. I didn't want to speak or be bothered with anything or anyone. I was literally in a funk due to my life being a virtual nightmare compared to how it used to be.

The day before Christmas, my dad made a relatively large amount of money from washing cars. Ironically, he was sober and in a good mood for a change. He decided to take me to the flea market to buy a couple of M.C. Hammer cassette tapes and a Walkman to play them on. The two M.C. Hammer tapes were called "Please Hammer, Don't Hurt Em" and "Too Legit to Quit." Back then, Hammer was my favorite artist, and I loved trying to imitate his dance moves every chance I got. This wonderful surprise started to break me out of the phase of depression I was in.

I started to think of all the wonderful things Santa had in store for me once I woke up on Christmas morning. We couldn't afford a tree, nor Christmas decorations, and we didn't have a chimney. Regardless of the circumstances, I just knew Santa would find a way to bring me presents, like he did every year. When we returned to our room, I fell asleep with my headphones over my ears while playing music all night (at least until the tape stopped). I woke up at the crack of dawn. While my dad was still sleeping, I looked around the room for the presents Santa dropped off, to no avail. There was nothing. I immediately lay back down and cried myself back to sleep. That's when I finally realized Santa wasn't real.

Apparently, my parents lied to me my entire life about old Saint Nick. I was beyond crushed. I didn't have anything—no mom, no sister, no presents, no Santa, no nothing. Nonetheless, I wished I had died right there on the spot. It was time for me to come to grips with my situation and fully embrace the fact that I was doomed to live that way for the rest of my life. What I didn't realize was that things would get worse sooner rather than later.

Nightmare in Miami (1992)

On a Friday afternoon, during the first full week of January, after getting out of school for the day, I returned to the house where we were renting a room. I attempted to unlock the front door with my key. After two unsuccessful attempts, I noticed the locks had been changed. I sat on the front steps while waiting for my dad to arrive. An hour later, the homeowner pulled up in the driveway and informed me that my dad's rental agreement was month-to-month and that he hadn't paid for January. I was dumbfounded at the moment because I couldn't figure out why this man was sharing all this information with me, as if I were an adult or something. It surely wasn't like I was a part of my dad's decision not to pay the rent. The owner asked me if I wanted to go into the efficiency to get my stuff, and I said, "Sure." When I got inside the room, I quickly grabbed my Walkman, cassette tapes, and the multiple bags of clothes we had. Then, I asked the man if I could wait outside for my dad, and he said, "Yeah!"

Around 8 P.M. or so, my dad finally arrived, higher than a kite with his eyes wide open like a zombie. It was as if he already knew what time it was. He didn't seem surprised at all by anything happening with our living arrangements. After he spoke with the landlord, we walked to 27th Avenue and caught the 27 (city bus) down to Liberty City. When we got off the bus on 69th Street, we walked to 70th Street and arrived at the Turf Motel. This motel was terrible looking!

Strange women were walking around with little to no clothes on, staring at us up and down, ending every other sentence with

31

"baby." "Hey, baby! Are you looking for a good time? I got what you need, baby." I was scared, to be honest.

When my dad and I reached the counter, I noticed that a bulletproof Plexiglas shield separated us from the clerk. My dad gave the man twenty-five dollars and received a key, two towels, and two washcloths in return. The clerk also informed him of the room's location, and there were likely extra towels available as well. As soon as the two of us made it to the room, we discovered the lamps barely worked, and roaches were crawling up and down the walls like they owned the place. I went from experiencing extreme fear to being extremely irritated. I repeatedly said to myself, "There's no way we can stay here overnight."

The next evening, things took a turn for the worse, since my dad used the remaining portion of the money he had on drugs again, and we had to walk from Liberty City to Carol City. In my adolescent mind, the predicament was worse since I didn't have a clue where exactly we were going. It seemed like a case of "the blind leading the blind!" Ironically, we ended up at the same location where I had witnessed him smoking crack before. Yes, the same dirty stairwell where I first witnessed my dad engage in drug use, near the 183rd Street Flea Market (in the same plaza as the Family Dollar, across from Burger King).

This trip was more unique than the last. We actually went all the way up the stairs this time (there was an old elevator there that didn't work). Once we reached the top of the stairwell, we discovered a locked bathroom up there. My dad told me to stay put, and he'll be back in a second. When he returned, he was struggling to drag up an oversized brown cardboard shipping box. Part of me wanted to offer some assistance; however, the intolerable part of me said, "He's the reason why we're in this foolishness anyway; let him figure it out." For the time being, I looked on with curiosity, trying to guess what he was about to do. Ultimately, he was able to bring the massive box upstairs. After accomplishing this feat, my dad closed one end of the box up and laid it sideways. Then, he took a pair of large white t-shirts from one of our bags of clothes and rolled them up to serve as bootleg pillows. Once my dad slid the makeshift pillows (made from T-shirts) into the box, he said, "Get in!" I looked at him like he had lost his mind and said, "Why?" He then said we were at the spot where we would be sleeping. The statement hit me like a ton of bricks. Afterward, we unfortunately got into a heated back-and-forth. After a while, I'd get in the box, as he originally requested. I asked him why we couldn't get a room at the Turf Motel, and he explicitly stated, "I messed up!" Then I asked, "Then why can't we just go back to Granny's house? He didn't answer me for some reason.

All in all, I was trying to stall and delay the inevitable. It was one of the most disturbing things I've had to do. The box was slightly damp, and I would occasionally feel the presence of an ant or mosquito crawling on my skin. I didn't sleep a bit! All I could do was lie there and quietly sob while trying to come to grips with the harsh reality that we were officially homeless.

The next day, when we woke up, my dad condensed the box and placed it in a corner of the hallway. All we'd have to do next was find a safe, inconspicuous spot to put our bags for the day. Conveniently, there was shrubbery around the building where we decided to put our bags. The only concern was whether the bags would still be there upon our return. We walked to the McDonald's on 183rd Street and swiftly went into the men's restroom. He then showed me how to take a "birdbath." A birdbath for us involved taking a good amount of paper towels from the dispenser, wetting them, and applying hand soap from the dispenser to them. Next, we would rub the paper towel together and create foam. Then we'd either take our shirts off or pull them up and quickly wipe our upper bodies off. We would take turns going into a stall and wiping our lower extremities with the same wet, soapy paper towels (it had to be ultra-fast to avoid being caught by other patrons or employees). This would be our routine whenever we slept outside.

As for food, on the nights when we didn't have any money, there were a few different activities we'd engage in. One of them involved us going behind the local KFC on 177th Street and raiding their dumpster for the food they would throw out overnight. My initial reaction to my dad's idea of dumpster diving for food was resistance until I discovered that, before the KFC employees throw out their remaining food, they package it up just like they would when selling it to customers. The food was even placed in huge plastic bags before it was tossed in the dumpster. Therefore, I didn't feel too bad about taking food out of the trash and eating it. (As long as no one saw me, of course) An old saying continued to resonate in my brain: "When you're hungry, you'll eat anything!"

We never sat and ate directly out of the dumpster. My dad and I would take what we could carry back to the area we slept in to avoid drawing too much attention to ourselves. Occasionally, my dad would use me as a lookout while he grabbed food from the dumpster. Come to think of it, he would also use me as a lookout when he was smoking crack, too. I felt like I was his accomplice every time I did it. Unfortunately, this became a way of life for me, and I hated it!

Hurricane Season (1992)

Going through homelessness during hurricane season was the worst. My dad used to always stay in the know about the local news and the weather.

When we were on the street, one of our frequent hangout spots was the Spin Wash & Dry laundromat on 182nd Street and 27th Avenue. This was the place where my dad taught me how to wash clothes. He would demonstrate exactly what to do, but I had to come by myself to clean anything I needed for the week. I remember the first time we went to the laundromat like it was yesterday. We walked in with a bag full of clothes, and immediately went to an available washing machine. We dumped the clothes in the washing machine and immediately headed to the customer service area to get the detergent we needed. After placing the detergent inside the washing machine, he would put the quarters from his pocket into the machine and push the lever back to start the cycle. I made a mental note of all the steps he took so that I could do the same one day. While the clothes were being washed, we would watch TV on one of the TVs in the corner, directly above the arcade games.

Fortunately, and unfortunately, this particular laundromat would become one of the staples of my childhood in Miami. Before I knew it, I was hanging out at the laundromat, even when I didn't have clothes to wash. I experienced many firsts at that place. It was the first place where I remember watching Michael Jordan play on television, the first place I remember watching the Dallas Cowboys, and also the first place where I washed clothes by myself. The Spin Wash & Dry laundromat was assuredly a safe haven for me, and the attendants who worked there never gave us a hard time.

One day, when my father and I were watching the local news, we heard about a terrible hurricane heading toward Florida. I was afraid, thinking to myself, "Where would we go and how would we survive out here if a hurricane hit?" The reason for concern was that a series of thunderstorms and tropical depressions had previously come and gone, and my dad decided to continue with our daily routines, as if the weather warnings weren't a serious issue. I guess he noticed the look of concern on my face as the news report concluded.

He immediately stated, "Don't worry, we'll go to your Granny's house if things look like they are going to get bad."

I was so happy because I didn't want to die or get seriously injured during a major storm. Hurricane Andrew eventually came and caused substantial damage to South Florida.

Before the hurricane made landfall in Miami, during the hurricane, and after it passed, we stayed at Granny's house. Surprisingly, I slept through the entire hurricane when it hit. The day after the storm hit, we went outside to survey the damage, and it looked like something from a war-inspired movie. Nearly every tree in the neighborhood was torn and ripped to shreds. Most of the power lines were down, but thank God, all the homes in the area seemed intact. The worst thing that happened to Granny's property was that the huge vine tree in the backyard was completely uprooted. This tree was one of the largest trees I'd seen, and everyone was so relieved it didn't fall on the house.

The disappointing part was that this particular tree was an attraction for my cousins and me whenever we visited Granny's house. We used to climb it and swing off its sturdy vines, pretending to be Tarzan every time. My relatives in the Richmond Heights area, located in the almost most southern portion of South Florida, weren't so lucky during the hurricane. The part of our family who lived in our town all drove down to "The Heights" to help our other family members with the cleanup efforts. Once we got there, there was total devastation everywhere. Power lines, rooftops, and trees were all over the place. Through the grace of the creator, both of my relatives' homes were spared from catastrophic damage.

Distraction (1993/1994)

Since my school was a K through 6, we were one of the few in Dade County who had a basketball team. On a whim, I tried out for the team, and surprisingly, after a hectic couple of days of tryouts, I made the final cut. Perhaps I was not one of the best on the team, and it was my first time participating in an organized sport.

The year before, I spent some of my downtime watching other people hoop around the neighborhood. I'd play pickup ball in P.E. whenever I could while at school. I would also go with my older cousin Lapolean (who was two years older than I was) and his homeboys from the neighborhood to various basketball courts in the area, such as Sherbondy Park and the one at Golden Glades Elementary. They would play against grown men and give them fits because they were so skilled at such young ages. I quickly learned the best way to sharpen your skills was to compete against older, more experienced people.

From time to time, I would have my cousin show me how to perform certain moves while dribbling. There were many occasions when I'd work on my jump shot when I spent time at Granny's house. Outside of practicing, I mostly learned by watching and mimicking more experienced players. I didn't have a basketball of my own, so I would borrow the one my cousin used to keep at Granny's house.

Along the way, when he was sober, my dad would show me how to shoot properly. Apparently, back in his heyday, he was a great athlete. Most of his peers from the neighborhood he grew up in shared many stories about how accurate his football passes were on the football field and how deadly his shooting ability was on the basketball court.

More Complications Along the Way (1993-1994)

While dealing with the mental anguish of going from sleeping outside and, occasionally, at the Turf Motel, being a part of my school's basketball team was most certainly one of the few bright spots.

An obstacle that was difficult to deal with was my overnight bladder issues. A few times every week, I would wake up soaked from urinating on myself. There were days when it was so bad that I had to go to school with soiled undergarments and clothing, especially when I didn't have clean clothes to change into. Before heading off to school, I would try to go to the McDonald's restroom and clean up as best as I could, but I would find out the hard way that the smell of urine lingers. I would get picked on and talked about often by my classmates.

There was one situation that occurred that struck me to my core. It was the day of a big game against Charles Drew Elementary, and Coach Aristide (our head basketball coach) told all the players to quickly put on their uniforms to prepare for the game. I used to wear my basketball jersey underneath my school clothes. Unfortunately, my undergarments reeked of the smell of urine from the previous night's peeing episode. Well, as a few of my teammates and I got into the back of our coach's pickup truck, one of them said, "Man, it smells like piss back here!" I immediately knew where the smell came from, but I attempted to play it off as if it wasn't me. One of them put their nose close to my jersey top and inhaled intensely and said, "It's Nando! He smells like piss!"

This was one of the most deflating ordeals I dealt with at the time. Externally, I tried my best to keep my composure and just laugh it off like it was a joke. Internally, though, it was a different story after the game.

When I returned to the spot where my father and I used to sleep, I cried until I couldn't cry anymore. For a while after, I was known as the kid who smelled like urine and wore the same clothes all the time.

***

New Norms

At times, I would not see my father until late at night. Our meetup spot after leaving school was usually the laundromat. I would often sit there and try to do my best with my homework. I'd also watch whatever was on their television.

From time to time, I would go to Granny's house until she resumed assigning chores for me to complete (raking leaves, cleaning windows, etc.). I used to wonder what my dad had going on, but I would just write it off, thinking he was out and about trying to earn money for us, as well as his detrimental drug habit.

When we were together, he would teach me specific survival skills just in case something happened to him. Some of the things he instilled in me consisted of resisting the temptation to walk down 27th Avenue late at night. 27th Avenue was one of the main streets that most people from Miami traveled down to get from point "A" to point "B." He would always tell me to take the back streets to hopefully avoid getting spotted walking all around the city by family members, friends, or associates of our family. He also taught me how to go around the back of the local flea market

41

and collect a bit of the freshly thrown-out fruit one of the vendors discarded. Another nifty trick my dad presented to me was how to steal cold-cut sandwiches from the local Shell gas station on 167th Street. The ideal time was always Friday evenings around seven, when a massive number of people entered to play the lottery, because the line always extended all the way out the door. The goal was to walk in casually and go straight to the refrigerated-goods section (which was located in the far-left corner of the store), open the glass door, and put the encased sandwiches in my pants pocket. At the same time, the cashier was busy dealing with the customers (who were normally chatty and distracting). This strategy worked one hundred percent of the time for me, and I was never caught. Some probably would say I was lucky, but I prefer "Trained by the best." The worst part about the entire setup was that there was a pay phone on the side of that particular gas station that my dad and I used on special occasions to collect-call my mom. I knew that if I were caught stealing from that gas station, we would have to use another pay phone somewhere else.

After a couple of weeks of borrowing money from friends and relatives, my dad would erratically leave me at certain times during the night to unintentionally fend for myself. I remember one evening when my dad left me in the laundry mat while we were watching Michael Jordan and the Chicago Bulls face off against the New York Knicks. During halftime of the game, he told me he'd be right back and left. I knew he was leaving to purchase drugs. One of the local drug dealer's houses was right off of 175th Street and 23rd Court. My stomach started growling, so I decided to go to a few backyards I was familiar with to take a couple of mangos (without the owner's permission, of course). Once my dad made it back to the laundromat, I had already returned, and I was sitting in the same seat he had left me in, with mango juice residue all over my mouth and t-shirt. He asked me where I'd gotten a mango from, and I told him, "Someone gave it to me."

Periodically, I would find myself telling little white lies out of nowhere, especially when my dad asked me questions. During this period, my dad and I expanded our horizons by trying out different places to sleep. Some nights throughout the year, some of those locations included abandoned restrooms in vacant buildings, the rooftops of vacant buildings, Gwen Cherry Park (once), and in a meter room. The majority of the places we slept were inconspicuous and helped us maintain a low profile.

New Mindset (1994-1995)

I was twelve years old when I started middle school, and I began to get the swing of the dos and don'ts of life on the streets of Miami. "Intimidated" was surely not the word I would've used to describe my interactions with street life at this point. I totally embraced all that my father and I had gone through, and I realized I had to start contributing financially to make our horrendous situation a little better than it was.

One Saturday morning, while my dad, Will, and I were washing cars at Consumer Meat Market (on 181st Street in Carol City), one of the Hispanic owners came outside and looked at me and said,

"Hey Kid, you interested in working inside on Saturdays? We need a bag boy."

I swiftly looked in my dad's direction for his approval, and he said, "Yeah, how much will he be getting paid?"

The guy said he couldn't legally pay me, but I could work for tips from the customers. My father and I agreed, and once a week, I would make anywhere from thirty to fifty dollars while somewhat relaxing in the air conditioning instead of in the hot sun.

I used the money I earned to buy Zebra Cakes, crunchy off-brand Cheetos, and Ritz sodas throughout the week. There were moments when I'd splurge and go to the candy man/candy lady's house (located around the corner from Granny's house) to buy frozen cups (frozen fruit juice in Styrofoam cups), hot sausages, and Cool Ranch Doritos.

***

While in school, I was still quiet and reserved. I didn't say much because I didn't want to give anyone an idea of what type of lifestyle my father and I were living. I made it a point to attend school most of the time to get decent meals, especially the free breakfast and lunch. A lot of times, after lunch, I would skip the rest of the day and go to Bunche Park, which was located around the corner from my school, North Dade Middle.

As a seventh grader, just about every single day, I'd avoid walking near certain kids because I knew I'd become the brunt of their jokes. Some of my peers would mention how they'd seen me walking down the street late in the evening. They were curious to know what I was up to and where I was going.

I remember there was a time when one of my teachers asked me what the deal was with me and my father. Come to find out, a few people used to see us walking at odd times at night. Off and on, we had to walk from 61st Street to 183rd Street if we didn't have the $1.25 for the adult fare and the 60-cent children's fare for the Metro city bus. There were a few times here and there when the bus drivers would let us ride for free, especially when they had sympathy for us due to inclement weather. There were also occasions when we would be offered "transfer" tickets by bus drivers if we told them we needed to catch multiple buses to make it to our desired destination. "Transfers" were discounted tickets that could be purchased on city buses to get on other buses that were to travel in different directions.

The Lottery Ticket (1994-1995)

On a Friday (during the first week of December, as school was letting out for the day), I remembered my dad had advised me to wait for him at Bunche Park until he arrived. He didn't get to the park until six in the evening. After he finally arrived, we went to Granny's house to help her move some heavy items around in her backyard. We finished around eight at night and received a nice home-cooked meal Granny prepared to thank us for a job well done. The food most certainly hit the spot that night: smothered pork chops, white rice, flapjack cornbread, and stewed okra.

As we left her house, my dad said he wanted to stop by Phillips gas station to "get some cigarettes." When we entered the store, he not only purchased the "Cancer Sticks" but also bought a one-dollar scratch-off ticket from the lottery. This was my first time witnessing my father pay for and play a scratch-off ticket. I've seen him previously play the "Cash Three," "Fantasy Five," and the "Play Four," but never a scratch-off.

As we were walking northbound down 27th Avenue, my father let out one of the loudest screams I'd ever heard. He was excited because he had won five hundred dollars on the ticket he purchased. We immediately returned to the same store where he bought the ticket and cashed it to receive his winnings. The celebration was short-lived because we didn't want to draw too much attention to ourselves, to the point where we could be followed down the street and robbed. I knew the first thing on my father's mind was to take the money he'd won to get drugs. While he did indeed go and purchase a few ten-dollar bags of crack, he still made sure that we went to the Turf Motel and paid for a room for us for a few days. He even surprised me by taking me to the Liberty City Flea Market on 79th Street. I was able to get a brand-new pair of all-white and red Adidas basketball shoes, along with a couple of outfits. One of the outfits was a white graphic T-shirt with Bart Simpson on it and green sweatpants, while the other was blue denim jeans and a white Polo shirt.

The following two days were some of the best days I've had in a very long time. My father took me to the Sky Lake Twin Theater at the Sky Lake Mall to watch two movies back-to-back.

"Finally," I exhaustedly stated to myself, "A chance to be a kid and take my mind off the stress of our situation. The trouble would start after the movies were over.

When we walked out of the movie theater, it was pretty dark outside, so I asked my father if we could grab something to eat, and he said, "Yeah, but you have two options: we can catch the bus back to Carol City and you can get a sandwich from McDonald's, or we can walk six miles back to Carol City. You can order a meal from McDonald's."

I became so mad, I could've cursed, but I tried my best to remain calm. At that age, I figured the money he won would hold us over for a while. I was sadly mistaken. Apparently, we were back to square one. My father nonchalantly told me the last of the winnings was spent on the movie tickets. As I was pondering what option to choose, a city bus pulled up and let passengers off at a bus stop no more than fifteen feet away from us. I looked at the bus, then I turned to my father and gave him a nonverbal cue with my head to indicate that I'd prefer to ride the bus than walk. It must've been fate that conveniently made the bus appear at that time.

Once we reached our destination, we stopped by McDonald's to grab a couple of McChicken sandwiches and asked for two small cups of water. My father told me he paid for the balance through "tonight" at the Turf motel, but the only issue was that we would have to walk there. So, we walked from 183rd Street to 70th Street. While walking in the direction of the motel, I kept thinking, "Maybe I should put myself out of my own misery by jumping out in front of the cars that are speeding by?" Yes, my ideas were morbid and downright disheartening, but I'd had enough of the torment! I wouldn't wish that way of living on my worst enemy!

Serpent at the Turf Motel

After a while, we finally arrived at the Turf Motel, and you wouldn't have known it was so late at night, judging by the number of people who were lingering outside in the parking lot. About ten to fifteen people were having the time of their lives drinking, playing loud oldie-goldie music, and smoking weed. The first voice I could recognize was Barry White.

Back in the day, my father used to go on and on about Mr. White's distinctive voice while we were sitting around listening to his old-school vinyls.

Honestly, the way the crowd was congregating, it looked like a family reunion. The usual "streetwalkers" were wandering around the premises as usual, looking for men to purchase their services. While we were on our way to our room, a few of the men gave us friendly head nods (a subtle way of using nonverbal communication to say, "Hello" or "What's up."). A guy who was staying in the room next to us was also outside, and it seemed like he was hanging out, enjoying the scenery. The guy said, "What's up?" to my dad, as if they had met each other before, but I didn't focus on that too much since I was fascinated by what he had in his hand.

The look in its eyes startled me at first. Before this night, I'd never seen one up close and personal. I couldn't even fathom why the guy was able to remain so calm with it wrapped around his right hand and forearm. It was a gray Burmese python! The guy turned to me and advised me not to be afraid. He said he was about to feed his snake a pigeon that was stuck in the gutter near the roof of his motel room.

He also said, "Hey, jit, you wanna watch me feed him?" (In South Florida, "Jit" was a slang term for kid, or someone smaller or younger than you.)

After processing the question for a second, I nodded my head in agreement to watch the muscular but odd-looking man feed his pet snake. All that kept running through my mind was how? The guy reached up and placed the intimidating specimen in the rain gutters located directly over our heads. This seemed strange to me because I didn't have a clue what he was doing. About a couple of minutes later, there was a burst of commotion that transpired above. The snake snagged the pigeon. The man reached into the low-hanging portion of the gutter and pulled the snake out, and I could see most of the pigeon's body in its mouth. As he laid the snake on the ground, it was slowly swallowing the pigeon whole. It was gruesome, yet interesting to see. To me, the occurrence was something new and mind-boggling, though to the owner of the python, it seemed eerily routine. I really couldn't believe what I'd just witnessed.

When I went into our motel room to tell my father what I'd seen, he was in the bathroom with the door locked and the shower water running. He even went as far as to take the extra towels in the bathroom and put them under the door for some weird reason. Initially, I thought he was just showering, but after an hour, I knew he was up to something suspicious.

When he finally came out, there was a strange, although familiar, odor that filled the room. It was at this time that I realized he was smoking crack again and not just taking a shower like I had naively been led to believe an hour ago. I didn't say more than two words to him at that point and just proceeded to grab my towel and washcloth to shower before bed. While in the bathroom, I put on my private investigator eyes to see for myself what he was doing for an hour, just to be sure. I saw an old cigarette cartridge in the garbage can near the sink (the foil was missing), and there were ashes or some sort of residue inside the toilet. This confirmed my suspicion!

After my quick and careful investigation of the bathroom, I took a shower and pondered on everything that transpired that day. I never knew I could experience so many different emotions in a 24-hour period; to say it was mentally taxing would've been an understatement.

Suicide Mission (1994-1995)

In August 1994, I'd recently started the seventh grade. There were certain special occasions when I would go to church on Sundays with Granny and Grandpa Theodore. She would keep a pair of my "church clothes" at her house, in one of the closets, in her spare bedroom. I would try to understand the religious words and phrases used by the reverend, Pastor McCrae, but for the most part, the messages always fell on deaf ears.

One message did seem to sink in, and that was, "If you call out to and seek God, he will come to you when you need him; he'll never leave you nor forsake you." So, for a while, I would try to speak to him, but I never heard anything in return.

I began to feel that all the spiritual mumbo jumbo was all talk and lies. I found myself attempting to pray every night while asking God why he was punishing me so much and why it seemed like he hated me. In my mind, if there were a God, I couldn't fathom why he would allow a child to go through what I was going through. I was completely filled with hurt, rage, and disappointment.

One Sunday night, when my father went off to "do his thing," I stood over the edge of the rooftop of one of the abandoned buildings we used to sleep in, hoping and wishing the lord would take me away from this horrible life, or I'd jump and end it all. But then, suddenly, I snapped out of it, and I uttered to myself,

"Well, if I jump, one of two things could happen: I could jump and die immediately and put myself out of my misery, or I could jump, survive, and, with my luck, paralyze myself. With the second scenario, I'd more than likely have to spend the rest of this worthless life homeless in a wheelchair."

Needless to say, I chose not to jump that night. To this day, I feel that if I had built up enough guts to jump and commit suicide, I would have, without a question. I guess another reason I couldn't go to such lengths was that I felt my father would probably try to kill himself if something happened to me. Regardless of how terribly things escalated, I told myself I would stick it out with him.

***

A few days after resisting the temptation to harm myself, I went to my grandmother's house, and she randomly approached me and offered to take me in, but I declined. All I told her was that my dad needed me. As more time went by, my dad would get entirely too comfortable engaging in his addiction around me. After a while, he wouldn't even attempt to hide it and would get high in front of me while I was watching, without thinking twice about it. I couldn't believe it. The man I've loved so much had turned into a monster right before my eyes. I wished there was something I could've done to help him see the error of his ways. I was learning the hard way, unlike the movies, wishes don't usually come true.

From Foe to Friend (1994)

While in the seventh grade, I started to converse more with my peers in class. There were a few fellas and one or two young ladies I occasionally spoke to. A young man I oddly gravitated to was EJ, in particular. He was kind of muscular for our age, but he had an annoying laugh I couldn't stand. We would crack jokes at each other often.

One day, when he came to class, he seemed to be having a rough morning. I decided to leave him alone, but one of our classmates pushed the envelope and bothered him anyway. He warned the young man to leave him alone, but to no avail. The young man continued to pester him until EJ hit him with a mean right hook to the temple. Once he hit the kid a few more times, I could see everything else happen as if it were occurring in slow motion. The kid got up and rushed EJ, who immediately scooped him up and slammed him into a desk so hard I believed he broke his back.

From that day forward, I decided it was in my best interest to become friends with EJ rather than an adversary quickly.

Death of a Loved One! (1995)

In 1995, my Aunt Teresa's husband, Melvin, died from his battle with an undisclosed illness. This would be the first death I was aware of in the family.

Uncle Melvin was a great guy whom everyone in the entire family loved. He and my aunt were like the urban version of Barbie and Ken dolls. They were the perfect tandem. Every time I saw them while visiting Granny's house, they were always upbeat, charismatic, and positive. Uncle Melvin was in law enforcement, dedicating his life to his family and serving his community.

When he passed away, it not only took a toll on the family but also completely devastated my aunt. I believe she was never the same afterward. I couldn't imagine the emotional toll it took on her to sit bedside and watch the man she loved more than life itself decline so rapidly. My Uncle Melvin was one of the few people who didn't pass judgment on my dad due to his addiction during those days. He was down-to-earth, and he tried to see the best in people, regardless of their situation or circumstances. Even in his passing, he ensured his wife was well taken care of, so she wouldn't have to worry about trivial things while he was gone.

Dream Team! (1995)

On an extremely humid Saturday morning, August 26 1995, we met Will at the Brands Mart, located off the 826 expressway and 187th Street. It was around 8:00 A.M. when we arrived, and Will told us there were a few cars and a truck to wash.

We wasted no time and immediately got to work. My dad rinsed the bodies of two cars with the water hose, and I filled the empty buckets with soap. We were like teammates; we all had an established routine that seemed to work to perfection. It reminded me of the teamwork I would see when I watched the Chicago Bulls play on television while chilling at the laundromat.

Will was the Phil Jackson of the operation because he ran the show and, in a sense, called the plays. He orchestrated the necessary work, determined the prices, provided the materials to complete the jobs, and distributed our pay at the end of the day.

My dad was the Michael Jordan of the group, since he was the self-proclaimed "best car washer" in South Florida. He would wash the bodies of the cars fast and efficiently. He was also a magician with a spray bottle filled with air freshener. Not only that, but he would also show me a trick to keep a car smelling fresh for weeks (spray the air freshener under the car mats and scrub the floor with a bristled brush).

As for me, I was the Bill Cartwright of the group; I was a dependable role player who stayed out of the way until I was summoned for assistance. My technique wasn't the prettiest, but I got the job done. My role consisted of cleaning tires and vacuuming out the interiors. I was pretty good at doing both, but I really enjoyed vacuuming, especially when customers left loose change under or in their seats. This was a habit I picked up from my dad. I'd often see him engage in this behavior, but I would act as if I didn't see him. I was unquestionably watching and learning from the best. I knew I had to do what I had to do to continue to survive. In my mind, the snacks I would buy with the stolen change were a matter of potential life or death from starvation. At the end of the day, we earned a pretty good amount of money, both legally and illegally.

Fed up & Fighting Back (1995)

I just knew we'd earned enough money to go to the Turf Motel for at least a few nights after the day of washing cars we had. We ate at a Chinese restaurant that evening, and afterward we went to the local "dope hole" so my dad could get his "Evening Delight." He left me on the corner of 170th Terrace and 25th Avenue because he didn't want me to go to the drug house with him. I sat there waiting for him for an hour.

While on his way to get me so we could go, he stooped down behind some sort of electrical panel/meter and took a hit of the drugs he purchased. He was a good fifty feet away from me, and he tried to make it seem as if he was bending down to tie his shoes. Maybe he tried to run game on me because he thought I was still young and naïve, but I knew he wasn't doing so because his "slip-on" shoes didn't have shoelaces anyway (they were the type of shoes Bruce Lee wore during his Kung Fu movies).

Out of nowhere, a man, seemingly in his late twenties, said, "Hey, you can't do that over here!" while racing out of his yard toward my dad.

He ran up to my dad and punched him in the temple and yelled, "I got kids over here; go smoke that shit somewhere else, get from around here!"

My dad stumbled a bit when he got hit; miraculously, he maintained his balance enough to scurry away.

After taking the blow to the head, my dad stated, "Alright, alright, you got it!"

There were mixed emotions on my behalf, since part of me was happy there was some retribution for my dad's actions, but the other part of me was embarrassed because somebody actually saw him using drugs out in the open. As we were walking towards the bus stop, I tried my best to contain my emotions.

I asked my dad if we were going to the motel that night, and he said, "No, I don't have any more money."

I side-eyed him and said, "What do you mean you don't have any more money? What happened to the money we made from washing cars?"

He vehemently stated, "It's gone, I do have some change in my pocket that I took from one of the cars we cleaned today."

After digging his left hand in his pocket to pull out the random coins, he inadvertently pulled his crack pipe out as well. He methodically took his right index finger and started to count what he had. When I looked down at the change in his hand and saw the pipe, something strange came over me. The pent-up rage inside my small and unimposing body had reached a boiling point.

I walked up closely to my dad and viciously slapped the money out of his hand. It felt like an out-of-body experience, and I couldn't do anything to stop it while it was happening. My anger had completely gotten the best of me. Some of the change abruptly hit my dad in the chest, and the crack pipe flew into the street. After noticing the mess I had made, I quickly took off running southbound down 27th Avenue. At that point, I knew I had messed up. I ran so fast down the street that somebody would have jumped to the conclusion I had someone shooting at me. There were many cars on the avenue that night, and I could hear car horns blaring from the people passing by while I was running for my life. I could also hear my dad in the background yelling my name while chasing after me. Under normal circumstances, I was considered slow as molasses, but I guess when a person's life is at stake, it enhances certain abilities. I was out of there, full sprint, nonstop. I ran from 170th Street all the way to Golden Glades Elementary, which was located on 165th Street and 28th Avenue.

The worst part about the situation was that it started raining. As I was sprinting, the freezing droplets of water hit me in the face, blurring my vision a bit. When I finally arrived at the school, I went to the far corner and used the smallest section of the wall along the south side of the building to help me climb to the top. Once I scaled the wall and lay flat on the roof, I made sure I was at an angle where no one could see me.

As fast as my adrenaline continued to pump, I could feel the rain start to increase a little, and I could hear my dad close by yelling my name repeatedly. I had to make a quick decision on my next move because I knew I couldn't hide from him forever. As I lifted my head to see where he was on the ground level, the rain increased, and it seemed he was about to leave the school grounds after many unsuccessful attempts to call out to me. That's when I cautiously stood straight up and said, "Yo, here I am!

"When I made my way down from the rooftop and walked toward him, he abruptly swung and punched me in the head, just like he had been punched earlier by the guy in the other neighborhood. When I fell to the ground, my face immediately hit a puddle on the ground. He fought me like I was a grown man that night. The pain from the beating subsided quickly afterward. I was more concerned about being filthy, soaked, and tired. Did I regret what I'd done? Not at all. If I were given the opportunity to do it all over again, I would've done so; on the other hand, instead of getting on the roof of the school, I would've run to Granny's house, which was right around the corner from the school. Instead of going to the Turf Motel, we walked all the way to 183rd Street and slept in the cardboard box that night. Our father-son relationship was severely altered after that incident.

Saved (1995)

In early December, as many of my peers were ecstatically gearing up for the two-week Christmas break, I was dreading the notion of going two weeks without the free breakfast and school lunch. Since I had already grown accustomed to my living situation and how I would survive without receiving proper nourishment from time to time, it wasn't like it was the end of the world to me. I was growing weary of having to fend for myself for so long.

It was currently my eighth-grade year, and there were a few days when I didn't see my father until late at night. I guess he knew that after all this time on the street, I was trained to survive and persevere through the harshest of conditions. For the most part, he knew my routine and I knew his, but one day something was obviously off.

The last Friday before the break, as school let out, I walked to Bunche Park to wait for my dad, as usual. Normally, I would walk to the laundromat and chill until he got there later, but earlier that morning, I remember my dad telling me to wait for him at the park after school, no matter what. I was tempted to leave once it got dark, but I wanted to follow the directions my dad gave me. While sitting on an old wooden bench beneath the pavilion, I noticed a familiar white van pulling up to the park, with a champagne-colored Honda Accord trailing behind it. It was Will hopping out of his work van, and my uncle was in a Honda.

Will came over, sat next to me, and said, "What's up, Marque?"

Instead of verbally responding, I merely nodded, bracing myself for the news to come. Before he could say anything else, I asked him where my dad was. He didn't tell me where he was, but he did say he's going to be gone for a while.

He also mentioned that my uncle and cousin were there to take me with them if I was okay with it. "If not," Will stated, "you can come with me."

I deliberated on it for a second or two and decided to go with my uncle since he was family.

As I made my way to the car, my uncle said, "What's up?"

I responded by saying, "Hey."

I wasn't really in the mood to exchange pleasantries. I was too worried about my dad and his whereabouts. Uncle Stetson begrudgingly said that my dad was somewhere safe, and he called him to ask him to pick me up from the park near my school. He also explained to me that I would be staying with him until my father could get his life back together. I was both shocked and confused. At least I knew that I was in safe hands.

My uncle was a high school teacher, and his son was a star multi-sport athlete. After getting into the car and driving from Bunche Park toward the rough areas of town, my uncle asked me where my clothes and other belongings were. After thinking about the question for a bit, I responded by mentioning that we kept our things hidden at a few different locations. I figured we would go to some of the spots to retrieve our things, but we never did. About thirty minutes later, we finally arrived at their house in Miramar.

As soon as I got out of the car and looked at the house, I suddenly felt a strange feeling come over me. For the first time in a long time, I felt safe. It was a nice suburban three-bedroom, two-bathroom house, with a one-car garage and a huge mango tree in the backyard. My great-grandmother also lived there with the two of them. Great Grandma Carol met us at the threshold of the front door and hugged each one of us as we came in. After exchanging a warm embrace, Lapolean showed me to the room I would share with him. I noticed there were two twin-sized beds (on opposite sides of the room), a few dressers, and a miniature-sized pool table with a television on top of it.

From the time I was picked up from Bunche Park to the time we arrived at their house, I kept my black Jan Sport bookbag on my back. Not knowing what to expect, I didn't want to make myself too comfortable, just in case something unexpected occurred. Two things about living on the street for so long: it taught me always to expect the unexpected and never to put anything past anyone.

After showing me where everything was located and reviewing a few expectations (that I wasn't listening to), Lapolean told me to take the bookbag off and relax. Before I could do so, Great Grandma came into the room and advised me to take a shower. When I took my shoes off, my cousin noticed that not only did my shoes have holes in the bottom, but my socks did too. He gave me an outfit and undergarments to put on once I finished showering. While I was in the bathroom getting ready to shower, he apparently asked his father what I was going to wear after today. My uncle responded by saying he would take us to the mall after I got out.

As for me, I took one of the longest showers imaginable, to the point that the hot water eventually turned cold. While we waited for my cousin to get ready, Uncle Stetson received a collect call from my dad, who was in jail. He gave me the phone after a few minutes, and I could tell he was relieved to be able to speak to me finally. He told me that he's f****d up right now, and he's going to get some help so we can be back together soon. Not only that, but he also told me he loved me and to stay with Stetson until he gets "back straight" again. He advised me that I should be hearing from him every week. After I finished speaking with him and my cousin got cleaned up, we got back in the car and traveled to the Pembroke Lakes Mall.

Now, at that point, all I was told was that we were going to J.C. Penney. I had no idea what or why my uncle was intending to purchase while there, yet I was in no position to ask any questions. I figured I was along for the ride. All that kept running through my head was the conversation my dad and I had on the phone before we left the house.

After arriving near the side entrance of the mall, we went into J.C. Penny, and my uncle looked at me and said, "Go ahead and pick out some outfits." I looked at him like he was speaking another language until he repeated himself with a swift and stern tone. Immediately, I went down several aisles, grabbing random articles of clothing, some that matched, others that didn't. A dose of excitement coursed through my body, and I couldn't believe what was transpiring. After grabbing what I guess I needed, we put everything on the counter, and my uncle handed the cashier a card to pay for all of our clothes. That was my first time witnessing anyone pay for something with a credit card. When the items were purchased, I vividly remember grabbing the bags as quickly as possible, as if they would be taken from me if I didn't act fast enough.

While in the back seat of the car on the way back to the house, I kept wondering if this was really happening. I surely needed time to process everything that occurred that day. I never would have imagined experiencing all of this within a 24-hour period. For some odd reason, I just knew that things would never be the same as before. The uncertainty of everything caused me to feel anxious, especially when I grew so accustomed to the route of the streets over the years. A stable living environment was uncharted territory for me, and little did I know there would be many bumps along the way.

***

Adjustment Period

Moving in with my uncle was, by all means, a huge adjustment for me. Not only did I have to grow accustomed to a new way of living, but I also had to suppress my emotions intentionally. With all the testosterone running rampant through the household, I didn't receive the chance to come to terms with all that I experienced over the past few years. Instead of learning how to be vulnerable and calmly expressing my feelings, I learned what it meant to be a young man based on our family's standards and to take care of business academically, athletically, and socially.

Thankfully, I was able to keep my insecurities and emotions in check most of the time as I went through this process. While living on the street for so long, one of the key strategies I mastered was blending into various environments to avoid drawing too much unwanted attention to myself.

In my new home, I tried to be "one of the guys" and follow their lead, but some things were harder to adjust to than others. One of the routines that was the hardest to adapt to consisted of waking up extremely early and eating a full breakfast. Something that seemed so simple took me a considerable amount of time to get into.

During the time my dad and I spent on the street, we never had the opportunity or the luxury of sitting down and eating a full breakfast together. We were always ripping and running. Other than eating breakfast at school throughout the week, my breakfast menu usually consisted of some variation of Zebra Cakes, Ritz Sodas, and Cheese Doodles (imitation Cheetos).

Therefore, sitting down as a family and having breakfast together was certainly an eye-opener for me. Many kids who have experienced what I went through would most likely appreciate waking up to good old 90s music blaring from the stereo and a plate of crispy salmon croquettes, thick and somewhat creamy grits, and delicious fried eggs. Not me, though. When I would be awakened earlier than I felt I needed to be, a grimace would instantly appear on my face. Every morning, for the first year of living with my uncle, this would be the new norm: wake up early, have an instant grimace, eat breakfast with an attitude, and then start my day. Rinse and Repeat.

It didn't take very long before my uncle and cousin noticed my daily demeanor during breakfast. With every day that would pass, I'd notice that they were paying more attention to my habits than I was initially aware of. They'd have some lighthearted fun at my expense, such as mocking my grimace and eye squinting while eating. The way they went about it was more than hilarious, but I couldn't let them see me crack a smile because it would encourage them to continue. I just went along with it. So, I would keep the grimace on my face, continue to give the appearance of an attitude for the rest of the morning, and go about my business like nothing happened.

Little did they know, I was no stranger to being picked on. Every time I was the butt of someone's jokes, it reminded me of when my dad and I were going through our rough patch. My peers would talk about my clothes, how I smelled, and my overall appearance. Externally, I knew how to keep a poker face. Don't get me wrong, though, the breakfast was indeed good. The problem was that I wasn't used to waking up so early, sitting at a table, and having a wholesome meal without looking over my shoulder or worrying about the day's events.

When I was on the street, I practically woke up whenever I wanted to, just in time enough to prepare for the day and make it to school for breakfast. There was no alarm clock or a timer. I guess I just let the spirit wake me up each morning. However, in my new home, things were entirely different. I had access to an alarm clock. Actually, my uncle was sort of a human alarm clock/timer himself because he not only ensured that we woke up on time every day, but he also set a time limit for us to eat breakfast so we could get to school well before it started.

Something else that was new for me was the car rides to and from school. My uncle and cousin always dropped me off at my new school, Carol City Middle, which was a minute or two from Carol City High, where they were going. My first few days at my new school were a bit contradictory to what I was used to. I went to school feeling good, looking better, with clean clothes, comfortable shoes on my feet, and also food in my belly. This was all new territory for me. To make matters even better, I even started to notice that I have caught the eye of a few young ladies in a few of my classes. Being the new kid on campus had its perks. The allure of the "new car smell" wore off after my first full week on campus, though. Once that time period passed, I became an afterthought for the young ladies. Nevertheless, the attention was cool while it lasted.

When it came to academics, I wasn't even an average student because the past couple of years of my life involved so much turmoil. I basically didn't have the time to focus on academics when my dad and I were in our situation. My primary focus was purely survival. Even though I was a below-average student, I always did the best I could to cover up all of my academic deficiencies. From the time I was in the fourth grade until the middle of my eighth-grade year, there were many times I had to resort to cheating on tests and guessing a lot. Luckily, I was never held back. (Either I was an expert cheater, or I was just superb at guessing.) One way or another, I was getting by, and I continued to use those same successful (depending on how you look at it) strategies at my new school as well. Seeing that I was able to BS my way through the Miami-Dade Educational System for so long, I figured, "Hey, why stop now? It's gotten me this far."

On the weekend, I would spend time with my dad after he successfully transitioned from the detox facility. Not too long afterward, he found a decent-paying job at the Airborne Heavy Maintenance Facility as an inventory control clerk. The maintenance facility was located near the Miami International Airport. My Aunt Teresa gave him Uncle Melvin's old car, a midnight-black 1987 Chevy Impala, to get from point A to point B. The car looked like something from a 90s action movie, and he appreciated her gesture. He was also currently living at a "halfway house" in Liberty City.

To me, it was a strange living situation. It was called a half house, and instead of a typical house, it was a miniature apartment complex. My dad was living in a two-bedroom, one-bathroom apartment. In his room, he had a roommate, and in the other room, two other guys were living there as well. He explained to me that all the occupants were recovering addicts, trying to get their lives back on track.

As I met each one of them, they'd share major details about their life stories with me. I realized they were trying to ensure I wouldn't repeat the mistakes they made in life. Afterward, I finally worked up enough courage to ask my dad what happened. He looked at me and asked me what I meant. I responded by asking him how and why he started using drugs. He looked at me and paused for a moment before saying that when we first moved down to Miami, he went to hang out with one of his childhood friends named Roger. They were supposed to be smoking weed, but his friend encouraged him to try crack cocaine for the first time, and he was hooked ever since.

"After that," he said, "I've just been chasing that first high ever since." He then emphatically stated, "That's all in the past, I'm off that sh**, and I'm getting my life back together now."

I was elated to hear and see my dad starting to resemble the man I remembered from his years in the military. Abruptly, before I could dwell in the feelings of happiness and get completely carried away, he told me he believed Granny and my uncle had something to do with his arrest. Unsurprisingly, he wouldn't go into details. I took what he alluded to with a grain of salt because I couldn't believe they would do such a thing.

My dad also shared with me how he had a rude awakening when he was sitting in jail for a few days. He was able to sober up and realize that wasn't a place he needed to be. When he was able to see the judge finally, he was given an ultimatum stating that either he could go to detox voluntarily or he would be released.

Still, the next time that he gets arrested for possession, he will go back to jail for an extended period. At that critical court hearing, with my grandmother and uncle present, my father agreed to go to detox. He told me that the reason he chose to go to detox was that he wanted to straighten out his life to get me back.

On the one-year anniversary of my dad remaining sober from drug use, he told me that he wanted me to go with him to get his "One Year" celebratory chip. That day, when I went to the Narcotics Anonymous meeting with him, I was able to meet his girlfriend, Jessie. She was pretty, although she couldn't have been any more than ten years older than me. Apparently, she was a recovering addict as well. I wasn't told much about her, but I knew she had made a few unfortunate decisions in life over the years. Jessie was very nice to me, and I didn't feel too uncomfortable about the considerable age gap between her and my dad.

When we arrived at Arcola Park, where the meetings were held, there were a lot of people there. They had light snacks and refreshments, which were delicious. When they called my dad's name to go up and receive his "One Year" chip, I was overwhelmed with pride to the point where I shed a tear. I was extremely proud of him. It was at this point that I knew he was really putting in the much-needed work to get his life back on track.

Later, we went out to eat at a local Red Lobster to celebrate. I remember it like it was yesterday. This was the evening that I ordered shrimp scampi for the first time. From the first bite, the taste caught me by surprise, and I was hooked instantly. I was so proud to be eating with my dad that night. He reminded me of the old version of himself —before the drugs, before the homelessness, before the discharge from the military. He cracked

71

so many hilarious jokes that evening that I couldn't control my laughter. Jessie and I both cried tears of joy while my dad was on his constant comedic rant. He even had the waitress unsuccessfully trying to remain professional and contain her laughter. It was nice to have an evening where everyone had the opportunity to let their hair down and just enjoy life.

High School Journey (1996)

Basically, after scheming my way through the rest of my eighth-grade year, I attended Carol City High the next year. I knew that I was in for a rude awakening, academically. My first week was horrendous; I didn't realize how severely behind I was. I tried to avoid drawing too much attention to myself by remaining as low-key as possible. Initially, I didn't say much to anyone until my cousin started introducing me to many of his upperclassmen teammates and friends.

After a while, a few of the boys from the football team started calling me "Showtime's Lil Cousin." When I was given this nickname, it allowed me to walk around with a sense of pride, like I was finally "a somebody."

My uncle played a major role in my first year in high school. Amongst the interesting classes I had, he made sure that I got into the school's Criminal Justice Program. This course was run by my uncle's friend, Mr. Antonio. The perks of this class included the potential to earn the right to partake in Dual Enrollment at Miami-Dade Community College for my eleventh and twelfth grade years, as long as my GPA remained at or above a 2.5. Mr. Antonio was an interesting man. He was a former police officer with the Miami-Dade Police Department. He would always have interesting stories about a perpetrator who went by the name "Willie Bobo."

Academically, the first couple of weeks of school were beyond terrible for me. All the tricks I used in the middle and latter parts of elementary school no longer worked. Participation was required, and the teachers that my uncle handpicked for me were no joke.

Consequently, I knew I had to get my act together and do my best to play catch-up as quickly as possible. So, from then on, to ensure I completed my assignments, I would go to the library to read and study. I studied extensively to try to play catch-up. I slowly covered ground with multiplication, basic division, and reading grade-level text. Understanding complicated terminology was also a struggle. It was a grueling and rigorous freshman year; however, I successfully persevered through it.

Thankfully, I came across a familiar face passing by in the hallway; it was my friend, EJ from North Dade Middle. When we saw each other, we swiftly smiled and gave each other a dap. To say that we were happy to see each other is an understatement. We caught up as much as we could before the warning bell for the next class period went off. Later that day, we'd locate each other at lunch and talk about the good old days.

Along with that, I also had a little spare time to try out for the basketball team. As far as the actual tryouts went, I did not feel confident enough in how I played at the time. Instead of going to both of the mandatory tryout sessions, I only attended the first one.

Around that time, I started to generate a little attention from a few girls who were in a couple of my classes. At this point, I guess I was finally "growing into my looks," if I don't say so myself. Surprisingly, this is where my cousin's expertise would come into play around that time. He was a junior and an excellent athlete who played football, baseball, and basketball at our high school.

Academically, he was a gifted student. He was also tremendously popular throughout campus. My cousin heard about the attention I was getting from some of the females around campus, so he sat me down and explained how I should deal with them when the time came. He provided me with pointers on what to say and how to say it. He would often try to encourage me to be a player and not be too quick to jump into any serious relationships. As a young man, I was fixated on finding real love. I didn't understand his angle at first, so I took his advice with a grain of salt. During the beginning stages of the conversations I'd have with the ladies, I'd try to play the cool role, even though I was the type who wore his heart on his sleeve. In a perfect world, that wouldn't be viewed as a bad thing, though in Miami, that's the sort of thing that often gets people in trouble. The reason I say this is that Miami is known as a city filled with vultures looking to pick people clean. When you're too kind, you often get taken advantage of. Regardless of this fact, my mindset was prematurely set on finding "Love," although I wasn't ready for anything serious.

When I spoke to females on the phone, my cousin covertly provided me with smooth, flirtatious lines behind the scenes. Sporadically, it would bother me, but most of the time, I was sheepishly grateful for the guidance because I didn't really know what I was doing. I believed the part that bothered me the most was the fact that the second-hand lines I delivered felt forced and inauthentic. During the occasions when I wasn't receiving assistance from my cousin, many of my one-on-one telephone conversations consisted of the following dialogue:

(Me) "Why are you quiet?

(Female Acquaintance) "I don't know; why are you quiet?"

(Me) I'm waiting on you to talk."

Most of the time, there wasn't much substance involved in my conversations back then. Sadly, I was a complete novice when it came to attempting to be romantic or charming.

Despite the age difference, my cousin was more like a big brother to me than a cousin, as he often taught me about loyalty, sports, females, and the importance of getting my life together.

***

Later that year, Uncle Stetson asked me how I'd feel about possibly trying out for the high school volleyball team. He told me that he was coaching the team, and he would teach me all I needed to know. Begrudgingly, I agreed to try out, and somehow, someway, I made the team. There were quite a few members of the school's basketball team who came to tryouts and made it as well. The majority of them were upperclassmen. Even though not many others tried out, I still felt accomplished, and it helped me gain a little confidence. It indisputably did wonders for my self-esteem.

It took me a couple of weeks to acquire the skills needed to compete at a high level. When I actually learned the game, I became an instant starter as a freshman. I was told that I was the first and only freshman starter in the last couple of years or so. I became a very good player because I constantly practiced and played intensely.

As a bonus, I ended up becoming friends with some of the other team members, who were also on the junior varsity and varsity basketball teams. Conveniently, I still found time to clown around a lot, to the point where the team started calling me Bay-Bay. This nickname originally derived from an animated movie called "BeBe's Kids." The comedy-laden movie dealt with little kids who were partaking in mischief.

Personally, I didn't feel that I got into much trouble, but I believed in having fun and would go to great lengths to have as much of it as possible. As I became more comfortable around my peers, I really began to act a fool while enjoying myself. I would intentionally play-fight and play practical jokes on my teammates, associates, and family members. I guess I was just enjoying life after experiencing so much turmoil when I was younger.

All in all, whenever I came around, everyone knew that I always had something up my sleeve. They would say, "Oh Lord, here comes Baybay," with a smirk on their face, while bracing for whatever they assumed I was plotting. After a while, I fed into the allure of my nickname, and I'd catch myself living up to the uncanny expectations that came with it. When my dad heard about how I was doing, he told me that he was motivated by the progress I was making both in and outside of school.

Church (1996)

On Sundays, my uncle would take me, Lapolean, and Grandma
Carol to our family's church home at Mount Tabor, located in
Liberty City. Most of the time, we would attend the early morning
service at 7:45 A.M. During that time, my cousin and I would go
downstairs to attend the youth bible study until it was time for us
to come up and join the adults for the pastor's sermon.

We often sat in the middle pews, even though Lapolean and I
always preferred to sit in the back. While Granny and Grandpa
Theodore were always sitting in the front row, I would marvel at
the giant hats and fluorescent dresses many of the women
Granny's age would wear. I preferred the back because I tended to
fall asleep during the long sermons Reverend McCrae used to
deliver to the congregation. I would always wake up with an extra
burst of energy whenever he started to get into his closing epilogue
and get everyone hyped with his spirited ranting and raving. It was
quite the spectacle every time, from the verbal cadence he held to
the physical bouncing in the pulpit, and the mastery of taking the
word of God and applying it to everyday life. I knew once the
organ player started pressing those keys, it was almost time to go
home.

The only part that I really despised was the fact that my cousin
told me that I couldn't take part in communion, since I had never
gotten saved. As a result, I wasn't ready to participate in the
fellowship with God to collectively acknowledge the redemptive
work of Christ on the cross. Upon hearing that from my cousin, I
knew what I had to do, though I didn't fully understand the
significance at that time. A few weeks later, in front of a packed

church, I made the shocking decision to go up to the front during an altar call. Honestly, I was scared, but I knew that I was long overdue. At one point, I reflected on all that God had delivered me from when I was on the streets, and I knew I was making the right decision by dedicating my life to the Lord.

While walking up to the altar, a young lady named Jackie from the youth choir immediately caught my eye. I was kind of ashamed to be thinking about a girl at a time like that, but I couldn't help myself. My hormones were racing faster than a racecar at the Indy 500. At the end of service, I worked up the nerve to approach the young lady and spark a conversation. She told me she was proud of me for taking a big leap by going up for the altar call. We exchanged numbers and started talking on the phone occasionally. Come to find out, we didn't live close to one another, so our only chance to really see each other would be at church, since it was (technically) the halfway point between where we both lived. She would eventually persuade me to join the youth choir as an excuse to see each other more than just once a week while at church. I knew I couldn't sing my way out of a wet paper bag, but I was willing to put myself through the potential embarrassment to see where things went with Jackie. I freaked out when members of the youth choir and I found out that we were requested to participate in an upcoming "Gospel Explosion."

The rehearsals leading up to the event would be held at nearby Mt. Carmel Missionary Baptist Church. I'd only make it to one rehearsal before skipping out on the whole choir experience. As time passed, Jackie and I stopped talking, and the rest was history.

Reconciliation (1997)

Every couple of weeks since moving in with my uncle, I would speak to my mom and sister on the phone, especially at the start of the school year. We were able to get in contact with each other through Granny. Come to find out, when she left Florida, my mom would periodically call her to check on me. Granny would tell her that my dad and I were living with her, even though we weren't. When my mom would ask Granny to speak with either me or my dad, she would always say we were out somewhere, doing something. She would inform me that she always found that very strange.

As the Christmas break of my ninth-grade year approached, my dad purchased round-trip plane tickets so we could visit my mom and my sister in Texas. He provided me with specific instructions on what we needed to do when we arrived at the airport, considering that this would be my first time on a plane that I could remember.

I wasn't scared to fly on the plane; my only reservation was potentially facing some of the possible pitfalls of flying. I was terrified of possibly falling out of the sky or something else dramatic happening to the aircraft. The turbulence reminded me of a news report I had watched earlier in the year about an earthquake that hit California. One guy who was interviewed described it as "seeing his life flash before his eyes." I could undoubtedly relate to his account. The way our plane was shaking and baking in the air, you would've believed we were on a ride at the county fair. When the plane finally landed, I was tremendously relieved; my dad, on the other hand, was cooler than an ice cube in a cup of water.

After obtaining our luggage from the baggage claim area, we went to meet my mom and my sister at the arrival section. When I finally saw them, it was awfully awkward. My sister ran up to me and gave me the longest hug, but my mom and I exchanged side hugs. My dad warmly embraced them as if nothing ever happened. Each of his hugs was long-drawn-out and overly dramatic. I assumed all was forgiven between our parents. Since we didn't have smartphones or FaceTime back then, this was my first time seeing them after they left Florida years ago. My mom looked the same way I remembered from back in the day, though my sister looked different. She was a mature version of who I remembered before. As soon as I saw her, I noticed that she was wearing prescription eyeglasses, which caught me off guard since she didn't wear or need glasses when we were younger.

When we got into our mom's car, I couldn't help but stare at everyone, off and on. It was unequivocally a surreal moment for me. I couldn't believe I was finally in the presence of the people who I felt had abandoned me when I was going through tough times with my dad. There was a lot of pent-up resentment that I never realized was there until we made it to Texas. We stayed with them for about a week and a half at their apartment.

While the first few days were smooth, my sister and I got into a series of minor arguments throughout our trip. Our first argument took place when she asked me what I went through when they left Florida. I lashed out because I felt that she and my mom were living a fabulous life, while our dad had me living a whole nightmare. Oddly, I placed more of the blame on my mom than my dad for some reason. I know it wasn't fair; however, that's the way I processed everything. Grace and our mom would respond by stating that I chose to stay with my dad instead of leaving with them when I had the chance.

During the week, we did a few fun things together as a family. All in all, we just tried to catch up as much as we could and spend quality time with one another. The day we left was uneventful; I dreaded getting back on the plane because of my previous experience on the way up. Before we left, my mom gave me a hug that was better than the shoulder-to-shoulder, half-hearted hug she gave me upon our arrival. While on the plane ride back, I couldn't resist thinking about all the events that transpired. Despite the many unsettling situations we experienced, I was still grateful to finally reconnect with them. It felt like a huge piece of me that was missing for so long was finally restored for a moment.

Social Life at School (1997)

After returning to Florida, I continued to adjust to life as a freshman in high school and enjoyed some of the perks of having an uncle and a popular cousin at the same school. I noticed that there was one peculiar female who used to stare at me every time we crossed paths. She would look at me as if she wanted me to talk to her, even though I was just a freshman and she was a senior. I won't lie, that alone kind of intimidated me a bit since I felt that I didn't have anything to offer her at the time. One thing led to another, and I eventually found the courage to talk to her.

Beforehand, I picked Lapolean's brain, and he advised me on what to say, and when the moment came, I forgot everything he told me. Therefore, I improvised and just spoke from the heart, and it was the corniest thing ever. I lead with, "Hey, what's your name? You gotta boyfriend?" What I learned in that situation was that if someone is truly interested in you, there's not much that can hinder you from at least getting their phone number. When all was said and done, we exchanged numbers and started talking every day. None of us had cellphones back then, so we would exchange house phone numbers.

In due time, she would show me the ropes and teach me how to kiss, and I'm not referring to basic kissing either. Honestly, I was a complete novice beforehand. I attempted to play it off and make it seem like I knew what I was doing, though she could tell what time it was. Initially, I was embarrassed, but then I quickly got over it and focused on ensuring that I got better every time we got together. Our weekly routine consisted of meeting up after school by the portables to spend a little personal time with one another until her ride came to pick her up.

After a few weeks, we both decided to discontinue the budding relationship due to our age gap, amongst a few other things. That was the first time that someone cried in my arms, and it made me feel terrible, even though the decision to split was mutual.

***

As the days passed by, I began to acquire a few friends around campus, especially in my criminal justice class. One classmate I formed a bond with in particular was Al. He was a sophomore at the time, and we'd talk about some of the girls in class, amongst other things. He was pretty laid back and unapologetically truthful when he spoke to people, which I could appreciate. I gravitated towards him more than others in the class because his demeanor reminded me of some of my family members.

 In each of my classes, there were some unusually funny characters, some quiet, and a few crazy ones as well. I fell into the quiet category in class, especially since my uncle worked there. He was the motivating factor in whether I chose to engage in the same shenanigans that some of my counterparts took part in.

Uncle Stetson was an intimidating force everywhere he went, especially at work. If you didn't know him and you saw him in a good mood, you'd think he was the friendliest man in the world. If you caught him in a bad mood or involved in a conversation that he was passionate about, you'd think that he had some bodies buried in the Everglades somewhere. The strange thing was that most people on campus knew not to try him, and when they found out I was his nephew, no one messed with me either. He was a "muscle head" who loved to work out at the house.

The loud grunting and clanging of iron weights would commonly wake my cousin and me up most mornings. Eventually, they would also start to have me lift weights with them in the den near the living room on the weekends. The stronger I got, the more confidence I'd begin to develop. As I started to feel stronger, no one could tell me that I didn't look the part, either. At times, I would flex shirtless in the mirror as if I had gotten diesel overnight, yet in reality, I wasn't getting that much bigger at all, just more defined. In my mind, I was also pretty sure that my physique wouldn't strike fear in any potential bully's heart at my high school. I would see smaller kids get bullied, but no one ever tried to bully me. Now, part of that could've been because of my uncle, and the other factor could've been my cousin, since he was one of the star athletes.

The football players were the alphas on campus, and people didn't usually bother them (nor anyone who was affiliated with them) too much. To make matters even better, my cousin and his teammates won their first state championship in football that year. So, when people found out who I was kin to, people at least took the time to speak to me occasionally. The great thing about it was that it helped me step outside my comfort zone and socialize a bit.

Life Outside of School (1996-1997)

Outside of school, in the Fairway community where my uncle's house was located, I eventually found other kids to chill with and play street football and basketball. Some of the kids that I'd cross paths with were Rod, Jermaine, TJ, Jahmash, Durant, and Ann, to name a few. Rod and his mom lived right down the street from Fairway Park, while Jermaine, Ann, and Durant lived on the same street as my uncle. Jahmash's grandparents lived in a house that was one street over from my uncle's, but TJ's house was about four streets over from there. The guys and I originally met while playing basketball at the park.

During the course of playing, they asked me where I was from, and once I told them that I was from Miami, they welcomed me into their unofficial circle. Apparently, TJ was from the inner city in Miami, and Jahmash lived in North Miami (frequently visited his grandmother in my uncle's neighborhood).

That day, I was playing some of the best basketball I've ever played, and when they asked for my name, I used my middle name (Marque) instead of my first name. I didn't want to give them my legal first name because I figured my middle name was cooler. I was concerned about whether I'd be perceived as cool if I let them know my name was "Fernando." One of them tried to repeat the name I stated, but instead said, "Mike," and I just went with it, especially since another one of them said, "Yeah, he had to have said Mike since he's out here hooping like Jordan!" It felt great to get a compliment from a peer, and it was then that I decided to let the kids in the neighborhood believe my name was Mike.

Now, when it came to Ann, she was the only female friend I had in the neighborhood. We met and exchanged numbers while I was just out and about one day. We became good friends, and we'd end up talking on the phone a lot rather than seeing each other in person. The conversations were never deep; she usually played reggae music in the background and quizzed me to test my knowledge of her culture.

Some of the things she'd ask me about, I was sort of familiar with because my uncle was half Jamaican. He constantly played a wide variety of reggae artists, such as Patra, Maxi Priest, and Shabba Ranks, amongst others.

Ann was cool, and I'd eventually meet her mom and her brothers at a holiday party they had at their home. We had a mutual platonic relationship that never overstepped boundaries, even though my cousin would eventually catch wind of the constant convo and ask me why I hadn't made a move yet. The people pleaser in me initially responded by telling him, "I was taking my time," even though she had already made it clear that she wasn't interested in anything but a friendship.

Occasionally, my cousin would feed me seductive lines to say to her, and she would call me out in a heartbeat. She'd say things like, "Why is your voice so low all of a sudden?" and "This doesn't sound like you; your cousin must be telling you to say these things." I'd be caught red-handed because I wasn't the best liar in the world, and those who really knew me could truly tell when I was trying to be deceitful.

One embarrassing experience occurred when Ann called the house to speak to me, and my cousin picked up one of the house phones before I could answer. I would usually and intentionally pick up quickly when I saw her house number on the caller ID to avoid my uncle, my cousin, or Grandma Carol answering, and Ann asking for someone named "Mike." Unfortunately, when Lapolean answered and she asked for "Mike," it opened a can of worms that I didn't want opened. I knew I'd have some explaining to do. When she asked for "Mike," my cousin said, "Who?" and, chuckling, handed me the phone. He said to me, "Why do you got this girl calling you Mike?" While putting the phone on mute, I talked to him about the mishap that occurred with the name situation. He told me that I needed to let her know that Mike wasn't my real name. Upon receiving the wise advice, I told her my real name.

I was ashamed, and I knew that I wasn't going to hear the end of it from my uncle once he found out. Surprisingly, once he found out from my cousin what was really going on, he didn't make a huge deal out of it. Eventually, he just told me that if anyone came to his front door looking for "Mike," he's going to tell them that no one by that name lives here, while shutting the door. I respected what he said. Nevertheless, I didn't have a choice, considering all he did for me, I wouldn't dare question anything he told me. Besides, he was probably the only man alive I was intimidated by.

Now, when it came down to Jahmash, that was my dog, my ace, and my riding partner. He and his family were of Haitian descent, yet he was raised and living in Miami at the time. He would come up to Broward County to hang out at his grandma's house to get a break from the Miami lifestyle.

He and I got involved in petty mischief around the neighborhood. We'd ride our bikes around the community looking for girls to talk to and other things to get into. While cruising down random streets, I'd have my headphones in my ears while jamming to Heltah Skeltah's "Nocturnal," Bone Thugs & Harmony's "East

1999," "Lost Boys," and "Legal Drug Money" cassette tapes. The only part I hated about the cassette tapes was having to abruptly stop my bike to take the tape out of the player and flip it over to listen to the "B" side songs. Every bike ride, I'd have different cassette tapes that I'd listen to. It seemed like each tape I would listen to would cause me to experience a variety of different moods. The Heltah Skeltah and Bone Thugs & Harmony tapes made me feel like the toughest young man breathing. The Lost Boys tape made me want to dance and vibe at the same time. I'd become a connoisseur of rap around those days. In my downtime, I'd watch music-based shows like Rap City: The Basement and 106 & Park to check out the latest songs.

When I would go visit my dad, I'd have him take me to the U.S.A. Flea Market in Liberty City, to buy the albums of the artists or groups that intrigued me. Jahmash and I would exchange tapes and compare the different types of music that we liked. One Saturday afternoon, he and I were bored, so we came up with the bright idea to climb onto the roof of a vacant house to chill. The house was located about ten houses to the right of my uncle's.

Once we made it to the top, we grabbed some gravel from the rooftop and tossed it into the canal directly behind the house. When we eventually climbed down, there was a police cruiser waiting for us in front of the building. Jahmash ran, and I started to run too, but I decided to give myself up because it wasn't like I was one of the fastest kids in the world, and I knew I'd get caught anyway. The officer said someone saw us throwing rocks from the rooftop, and they called the police. He then asked me who the other kid was who ran and where he stayed, and I didn't respond. Then the officer asked me if I lived in the area, and this time I decided to answer by informing him that I did indeed live down the street. It was then that he whipped out the brightest handcuffs I'd ever seen and told me to place my hands behind my back. Once he put the impressive-looking set of handcuffs on my wrists, the officer told me to get in the backseat of his patrol car. This was my first time experiencing getting detained by the police, and God oh mighty was I terrified. I wasn't concerned with possibly going to jail. I was more scared of the possibility of facing my uncle.

The officer drove me down to my uncle's house, and when we arrived, without a doubt, I didn't want to get out of the car. As we were walking up the driveway, I was saying silent prayers, anticipating and bracing myself for whatever harsh punishment he would have in store for me. When we got to the front door, the officer rang the doorbell, and my uncle came to the door with a confused look on his face. The officer asked him if I lived there, and my uncle said, "Yes, that's my nephew." Immediately, the officer told him what I was detained for and that he needed to do a better job of keeping an eye on me. While he was talking to my uncle, he was simultaneously taking the handcuffs off me.

When I got in the house, I was expecting to get swung on, at least, but it never happened. As a matter of fact, he didn't say two words to me. He made a beeline straight for his room and slammed the door. It was easy to tell that he was disappointed in my actions, and I also figured that he spared me that day. He probably wanted to kill me. I couldn't really say I'd blame him if he actually felt that way. He left the rest of the tough conversations to his son, maybe because he knew that if he spoke to me about the previous situation and I said the wrong thing or even looked at him crazily, he'd knock my head off.

Unknown Ability (1997)

In June 1997, prior to the beginning of my sophomore year, my cousin had me accompany him to the local park to help him complete some football drills. He wanted me to throw the ball to him so he could work on his catching ability.

As I stepped back to throw the brown, seemingly oversized football, I clenched my teeth and threw it as hard and as accurately as I could. A second later, he catches the ball and pauses for a minute straight while staring at me aimlessly. He threw the ball back to me and told me to throw the ball to him again. I repeated the same throw as before, and after catching the ball again, Lapolean said, "Damn, you can throw the ball, cuz!" I looked at him and smirked, confused, since I didn't have a clue what he was talking about. Then he proceeded to inform me that he'd be running "routes," and toward the end of these routes, he'd tell me when to throw the ball.

After an hour of completing these drills, my throwing arm/shoulder was so sore that I could barely lift my right arm without feeling pain. Regardless, I was honored to be helping a current state championship winner work on his craft. I figured the temporary pain was worth it since he was being heavily recruited by many of the top college football programs in the country. Little did I know that he would come up with the bright idea for me to attend summer workouts with our school's football team. Honestly, I wasn't too thrilled about the possibility of playing organized ball, considering that I'd never played previously. My cousin told me not to worry about anything and just to give it a try to see how I'd

91

do. I successfully went through summer conditioning, weightlifting, and other football-related workouts.

When Granny caught wind of me potentially playing football, she grew overly concerned. She told me that she didn't feel it was a good idea since I was born with the trait of sickle cell. She also told me that, physically, I may not be able to do what everyone else can do.

I didn't understand the significance of what she was trying to say until my dad told me that his deceased sister, Lisa, died from full-blown sickle cell anemia, before I was born. I attempted to understand things from Granny's point of view. Due to my ignorance when it came to understanding what a trait of sickle cell consisted of, I disregarded the concern and decided to continue pursuing my athletic endeavors, regardless.

At the end of the day, my grandmother was just being a caring individual, and her statements actually motivated me to participate in many extracurricular activities. I guess it's safe to say that I wanted to prove that I could do anything and everything other kids could do, regardless of the circumstances.

***

My tenth-grade year was an extremely busy one. Somehow, I made the Junior Varsity (J.V.) football team as a backup quarterback, and I was also placed in all honors classes based on my freshman year's grades and test scores. I didn't realize how big those achievements were for me because I became fixated on how hard everything would be instead of focusing on how far I'd come.

As far as football was concerned, I was worried about remembering the plays, getting hit, and potentially letting the coaches down. I was also so concerned with everyone's perception of me that I didn't enjoy much of the junior varsity season. Thankfully, EJ was the starting running back. He was one of the people, outside of my cousin, whom I could confide in. My jersey number was thirteen, but my skill set was the furthest thing from the Miami Dolphin's All-Pro Quarterback, Dan Marino (also #13).

One of the few things I liked during the season was getting the chance to learn from the star senior quarterback, "J." He was a real-life legend in the community after leading the team to a state championship last year against Hillsborough. He would show me and the other J.V. quarterbacks how to properly warm up and work on throwing mechanics. Occasionally, while comparing myself to the other quarterbacks, I'd notice that the majority of them were bigger, more talented, and more knowledgeable about the game of football. I knew that I was out of my league from the initial onset of the season, but I had to remain calm and keep my poker face on constantly.

During each practice, I would try my hardest to remember what to do and how to do it. Thankfully, the head coach loved calling run plays instead of passing plays. The run plays weren't as difficult for me to remember, but the pass plays had many variables that I had to consider. When it was my turn to work on plays with the offense, I would perform pretty well—until it was time to pass the ball, that is.

When I was helping my cousin work out during the summer by throwing the ball to him, it seemed easy; however, I would come to find out things were totally different when it came down to throwing a football with shoulder pads on. It felt so uncomfortable to do. I wished I had the opportunity to practice without them on, so I could show everyone how well I could throw the ball. Eventually, a few of the upperclassmen would make fun of the fact that I wasn't a skilled passer and refer to me as "Slingshot." The entire situation certainly destroyed the little bit of confidence I'd accumulated from last year. I kept telling myself that as soon as the J.V. season was over, I'd never play football again. It's a secret that I would strive to keep to myself until the time was right.

During the season, I only played in a couple of games, yet there was one game in particular that I'll remember for the rest of my life. We had a game at Hialeah Miami Lakes High, and while getting dressed, I absentmindedly forgot to put my butt pad in. Towards the end of the game, I was put in during the last drive. It was a designed run play (33 dive-dive) for the running back that the coach called, but I knew once the center snapped the ball to me, I was going to keep it and take off up the middle instead. I was so nervous and scared, to be honest, I just tried to run as fast as I could when the ball was snapped. Then that's when it happened; one of the defensive linemen on the opposing team unintentionally drove his helmet into my tailbone. My adrenaline was rushing so much that I wasn't able to focus on it too much. It wasn't until we got on the bus headed back to our school that I noticed the most unbearable pain that I've ever felt in my life.

My tailbone was literally on fire. Sitting down on the seats was virtually impossible. I was determined not to let my teammates know about the embarrassing ordeal, so I endured as much as I could, trying to prop myself up with my arms while barely touching the seat in front of me. For the most part, it worked until we hit speed bumps or crossed railroad tracks. It was rough. When we finally arrived at our school's locker room to change out of our uniforms and go home, I moved so gingerly that many of my teammates kept asking me what was wrong, and I'd respond by telling them I was alright. While waiting for Uncle Stetson to pick Lapolean and me up, I told him what happened at the J.V game (the varsity had practiced at our school while we were playing our away game), and he said, "Damn, cuz, I know that's got to hurt," and he chuckled. I chuckled as well because it sounded like a silly injury that could've been avoided had I just put my butt pad in before leaving for the game. I had no one to blame but myself.

Getting in the car once my uncle arrived (after an hour or so) was a huge task. It was the type of pain that I wouldn't wish on my worst enemy. When we got home, I promptly went to the bathroom and checked my backside, and I saw a black bruise on my tailbone. The bruise and the pain lasted the entire week. At home, I had to resort to lying on my belly, and in school, I had to grin and bear the pain in each of my classes.

After the last J.V. game of the season, I went into the locker room with the biggest smile on my face because I knew I wouldn't be back. Mentally, I was already preparing to attend the last session of basketball tryouts, which most of the football players interested in playing would normally attend. Suddenly, I heard a stern, aggressive voice yelling my name from the head coach's office. I walked swiftly as I arrived at the threshold of the office door. I saw Coach Legend (with a lit cigar and his train conductor hat on), and he told me that I will be moving up to varsity for the playoffs to gain experience for next year. Externally, I appeared to be happy and appreciative; nonetheless, internally, I was hotter than fish grease. I couldn't believe it. It was bad enough that I barely played on junior varsity, but this man had the audacity to tell me I was moving up to varsity. I told myself that someone must be pranking me until I attended my first day of varsity practice. I wasn't scared; I was mortified. I would hear some of the players having sidebar conversations, asking each other, "How'd he get moved up?" The coaches did their best to coach me up and not put any pressure on me.

Every evening after practice, there were a few of my cousin's homeboys who would offer words of encouragement. Certain players, such as EJ, O.J., Brice, and Metri, were some of the guys who'd try to be positive by telling me to keep my head up and continue to work.

The first two playoff games were so nerve-racking. While standing on the sideline, I can recall watching the scoreboard, hoping the games weren't complete blowouts so the coaches wouldn't put me in. During one of those games, I remember Granny yelling my middle name out loud, attempting to get my attention. She would yell, "Marque...Marque... It's your Granny! I know you hear me calling you! Don't make me come down there!" It was so embarrassing because the crowds at our games were astronomical. Eventually, I'd turn around quickly and give her and the rest of the family a swift wave. Afterward, I'd turn back around to act as if I was locked in watching the game.

After our team beat all of their local rivals, we had a full week and a half to prepare for the state championship game in Lakeland. There was one practice where I was actually called upon to participate in a few plays. Before this specific day, I'd usually stand and watch when the team "went live." The first play was a simple handoff to the running back, but the second play was supposed to be a tight-end pop pass; I had to deviate since the defensive linemen were converging on me. I frantically scrambled and made a perfect twenty-yard pass downfield to a wide receiver nicknamed "Pistol." Coach Legend was ecstatic. I remembered him saying, "There you go, boy!!!!" "That's what the hell I'm talking about," as he slapped my helmet. That was the proudest, not to mention luckiest, moment that I had while on the team. For a split second or two, I almost felt like I really belonged. Towards the end of practice, I noticed that my cousin and the starting quarterback weren't there at all. I overheard some of the coaches discussing how the two of them got into trouble at school, which resulted in them being kicked off the team.

Right after practice, I got dressed and headed over to the gym to watch the girls' and boys' varsity basketball teams play. When I got to the gym, I saw my cousin speaking with a group of dudes; I didn't want to interrupt, so I said, "What's up?" to a few people I knew from class and sat down in the stands while the girls' team warmed up. To take my mind off the football drama, I focused my attention on one of my friends, Stephanie, while she was getting her warm-up shots in.

***

When she saw me, we gave each other a subtle head nod to acknowledge one another. Steph was in a few of my classes during the day, and she was hilarious. We had occasional conversations from time to time, and she would do intentional flirtatious things to get me to fall for her. She'd also invite me to some of her home games to make her older boyfriend, Julius, jealous. She had no idea that I knew what her intentions were, but I did. I wasn't a complete idiot, even though I played the role well. Little did she know, I heard rumors that Julius was messing with girls from other high schools, and I knew she was using me for payback for something he'd done, which didn't bother me that much. We never talked about any of that. I was cool playing her little game. I was just happy that someone attractive and popular acknowledged my presence, not to mention she was pretty good at playing my favorite sport, too.

After the girls' game was over, my cousin came to fill me in on what was going on with everything. Suddenly, Steph came up into the bleachers, hugged me, and sat between my cousin and me. I

97

told her she had a good game, and then we spoke for a few seconds. While we were talking, she said she was hungry, and I looked at my cousin out of the corner of my eye. He slid me a couple of dollars in an inconspicuous manner so that Steph couldn't see. After receiving the money, I gave the bills to her and said, "Here, go get you something to snack on," and she took the money and asked me if I wanted anything. I responded by saying, "No, I'm good." When she left to go to the concession stand, in the back portion of the gym, Lapolean slid close to me and asked me if I knew she was Julius's girlfriend. I told him that I did, but that didn't have anything to do with me because we were just friends. He looked at me, smiled, and gave me dap to acknowledge the fact that I was growing up while completely throwing caution to the wind.

A few seconds later, Steph's boyfriend and the boys' basketball team entered the gym, and as she returned with something to drink and a pack of Skittles, she sat extremely close to me. This was something I hadn't experienced too often, so I tried my best to contain my excitement and play cool for the moment. When Julius looked up in the stands and saw how close she was to me, it was apparent that he was visibly upset. The anger was written all over his face, and he seemingly channeled that anger to play one of his best games. I knew if anything confrontational occurred after the game, my cousin always had my back.

Toward the latter part of the game, as Steph got ready to leave the gym to walk home, she hugged me while I was still seated and seductively slid her hand across my right knee as if I didn't know what she was trying to do. When the game ended, my cousin and I walked toward the concession stands, and a group of guys stopped him to ask about the rumors of him and J getting kicked off the team. While he was explaining the situation, I heard some of the other varsity football players talking with their partners about the quarterback situation. What stuck out to me the most was one kid asking the players, "Who are the backups to replace the starting quarterback?" They mentioned Ed and Metri, then looked in my direction and said, "Oh hell no, not Slingshot!" One of them also mentioned that Metri was no longer eligible to play because of his grades. I immediately tried to act like I didn't hear them as I walked out of the gym. All I could think about was that if our starting quarterback couldn't play and our backup got hurt, I would potentially be the only option.

Later that night, I freaked out. I just knew I had to get myself out of this potential nightmare of a situation. I told myself that I would have to come up with an excuse not to travel up to Gainesville when the team hit the road for the state championship.

* * *

The next day after practice, I bravely went to Coach Legend's office door and knocked lightly. At first, he didn't hear me, so I knocked a little louder, and he told me to come in. I apologized for bothering him at that moment and told him I wouldn't be able to travel to Gainesville with the team.

As I expected, he swiftly asked, "Why not?"

I stuttered a bit and told him that I'll be leaving the team to start working on my skills in hopes of making the basketball team.

Coach Legend sat up in his chair and said, "If that's what you want to do, go ahead; I won't stop you; I think you've gotten better since we decided to move you up to varsity.

I was honest with Coach, and I told him I was more of a basketball player than a football player. I thanked him for the opportunity as I walked out of his office. I went to the locker room when no one was around and cleared out my locker. I felt like a weight was lifted from my shoulders.

A small part of me felt like a quitter, though; however, I got over that expeditiously. When I made my way toward the student parking lot, Lapolean was standing near the railing where all the "who's who" of Carol City gathered after school, waiting for their girlfriends to finish various practices. I casually dapped him and the rest of the boys up.

While doing so, I heard one of the other football players say, "Congratulations" to my cousin for getting back on the team. I wondered what happened and how he was able to rejoin; however, I couldn't bring myself to ask in front of all his peers, as everyone there was a year or two older than I was. I didn't want to come off as overly nosy and immature. He did state that J had just gone back to Coach Legend's office to attempt to get back on the team as well.

The strange thing about it was that when I was leaving his office, I didn't see J walking past me. I must've missed him during the excitement I felt after my heart-to-heart with Coach. A few minutes later, we all found out that J was also allowed back on the team, and all seemed right with the world again. Then, suddenly, one of the boys asked me if I was ready for the trip to Gainesville, and I knew I couldn't tell them the truth because I would have been clowned by anyone who knew me for quitting.

I immediately said the first thing that came to mind: "Coach Legend told me that they didn't have enough room on the bus for everyone, so I won't be able to make the trip with y'all."

My cousin and the rest of the boys were like, "Damn, that's messed up!" "You've been practicing and putting in work like the rest of us; you deserve to go!"

When I sensed a potential issue arising from the lie I had conjured up, I had no choice but to attempt to de-escalate the situation. I started by telling them that I was ok with not going to the state championship game since I was tired of waiting to start working out in preparation for volleyball season and next year's basketball tryouts. They looked at me like I was stupid and laughed hysterically. Until the time Uncle Stetson arrived to pick my cousin and me up, they cracked jokes on me and then on each other to pass the time. When we got in the car, Lapolean told his dad that he and J were back on the team, and he also spilled the beans about my embellished story.

Even though I didn't end up going with the team to the state championship game, our entire family made the trip to support my cousin and the rest of his teammates. Our football team eventually won the thrilling state championship game against Lake City Columbia, 20-17, after falling behind 6-17 at halftime.

***

Public Embarrassment

At the conclusion of the football season, since my name was still listed on the final championship roster due to practicing and being on the team during the playoffs, I was able to attend all the celebratory events sometime after everyone returned to town.

As we were gearing up for the championship parade the day before, Lapolean drove us to get haircuts in Liberty City from my uncle's childhood friend Edward. Edward was a cool dude who resembled a funny-looking version of Jamie Fox, with glasses.

When he was cutting our hair, he seemed distracted by his conversations with everyone, and the result was traumatic for us. When we returned to the car after getting our cuts, we looked in the mirror, and we couldn't believe what we were looking at. He'd given us "Super Bowls!" A Super Bowl (the haircut was really known as a Soup Bowl; unfortunately, in the hood, we liked to rename things all the time) was known as one of the most embarrassing haircuts anyone could have. It literally looked like someone stuck a bowl on top of a person's head and cut around it.

I was in tears just thinking about the ridicule we'd face from the rest of the football team once they saw our haircuts. As soon as we got home, we swiftly grabbed the clippers from my uncle's bathroom, and Lapolean tried to fix the blend of our hair, to no avail.

The next morning, when I woke up, my cousin was gone. He borrowed his dad's car and went somewhere without a single warning. After I got up, I decided to get my outfit together in preparation to attend the parade. When he finally returned home from whatever mystery location he had ventured off to, it looked as if his hair was perfectly blended all around. I couldn't believe my eyes... the first thing that came to mind was, "I know this man didn't go get his hair fixed and didn't take me with him."

When I asked him who cut his hair, he sheepishly told me, "J did," and that he tried to wake me up to see if I wanted to go, and I wouldn't wake up. He also mentioned that J was in a rush, so he had to arrive by a certain time and couldn't wait. Apparently, J wasn't only our high school football team's quarterback; he also cut hair on the side. After finding out how he was able to get his hair fixed, I really felt a certain way. Knowing that there was nothing I could do, I just kept it to myself, since I wasn't the confrontational type. If I were a fighter, we would've been throwing hands on the spot.

We'd eventually make it to the meet-up spot where the entire football team was supposed to meet to find out what we would be doing during the parade. The boys and a few of the coaches took one look at my haircut and instantly started to crack jokes. Some not so funny, some hilarious. All I could do was laugh it off and give my cousin one of those "I can't believe you set me up for this ridicule" faces. We found out that we would be on fire trucks throughout the parade, and it would be televised, too. My luck couldn't get any worse.

Throughout the parade, I attempted to hide my face as inconspicuously as I could. Something told me that someone would spot me no matter how hard I tried to remain low-key. A day or so later, one of my other cousins from Richmond Heights called me and said they saw me on television while watching the news, and then they began to talk about the parade. I'd eventually be taken to another barbershop by my dad, to have my hair fixed a few days later. That would be the last time I'd allow anyone to cut my hair while I was in high school.

***

Championship Celebration

Weeks later, the next celebratory event was the team dinner at Don Shula's Steakhouse in Miami Lakes. During this event, everyone would be getting their state championship rings and lettermen jackets. I was told by the coaches that I wouldn't receive a state championship ring because I left the team before the state championship game, but I would receive a state jacket since I was on the team throughout the playoffs. I was cool with the concept, since I initially felt that my lackluster performance on J.V. should've been grounds to not move me up to varsity anyway. I think I started to buy into the daily schoolhouse gossip that I was lucky to be elected to move up for the team's playoff run because of the circumstances surrounding the other quarterbacks on the team.

When I finally received the impressive-looking orange jacket with black leather sleeves and tried it on, I felt a bit nervous and somewhat apprehensive. I couldn't help but wonder if the coaches viewed me in a negative light since I quit the team. Thankfully, no one there questioned why I didn't travel with the team to the championship game, and to this day, I still don't know if Coach Legend ever shared the particulars of our conversation with anyone.

Days later, when returning to school, most of us wore our team jackets, and I was so proud to feel like I was finally a part of something important, with a smile on my face the entire day. Occasionally, I'd hear a couple of haters make comments about me having a championship jacket when I didn't play one snap on varsity. However, I'd let those comments go in one ear and out the other. That jacket became one of my most prized possessions for years to come.

As for my cousin, he received many accolades, including being selected to play in the annual Florida versus Georgia All-Star football game and the annual Dade versus Broward game. He was also acknowledged as an All-State Defensive Back and later went on to Florida State University to continue his football career.

Basketball Junkie! (1998)

After the 1997-1998 football season, I fully submerged myself into all things related to basketball. I even attended the special tryouts held by the basketball coaches for any interested football players to see if I could be a late addition to the team. I knew I didn't have a chance since all of my time was previously dedicated to football. Furthermore, I hadn't practiced or played basketball consistently in a while. I decided to give it a shot anyway, to see what I needed to work on.

After not making the team, I'd eat, sleep, watch, practice, and play basketball every day in hopes of improving my overall skill set. I was overly determined to make the basketball team the following year, so I decided to fully commit to my own personal development, both physically and mentally. Not only that, but I knew my ball-handling/dribbling ability wasn't the best, so I would work on that skill every day after school in the neighborhood. I would dribble everywhere—the street and the driveway, as well as to Fairway Park.

Even on the weekends when I would visit my dad, he and I would go to a few of the local parks in Liberty City and play basketball against random guys. My dad had a picture-perfect jump shot that I struggled to mimic. My jump shot was a bit unorthodox and streaky at best, yet his was silky smooth and consistent. I also increased my weightlifting regime. Pushups, bench pressing, lateral pulls, and bicep curls are a few of the exercises that I'd partake in at my uncle's house two to three days a week.

Toward the latter part of the year, I would make the varsity volleyball team again. I started every game and became a leader on a team that was good enough to finish the season with a better record than the previous year. Volleyball slowly started to become one of my favorite sports to play. The teammates I had who were also on the basketball team would refer to spiking the volleyball as slam-dunking on the opponents. In turn, this concept would encourage all of us to seek out highlight-worthy spikes during games to get the entire team excited and motivated to remain competitive throughout the season. When one of us would spike the ball on an opponent, we would celebrate as if we had won a championship. There were a few times when we caught the referee smiling or laughing as we acted a fool on the court. They always knew that we didn't have any ill intent; we were enjoying the sport as young inner-city youth. Those were really fun times.

During and after volleyball season, I stayed involved in basketball outside of school. Academically, I continued to flourish, although I never lost focus on my overall goal of making the basketball team. It became an obsession after a while. That summer was pretty productive for me, and my dad even paid for a round-trip flight so Grace could spend a couple of weeks with us. Since she couldn't stay with our dad at the halfway house, she occupied one of the extra bedrooms at Granny's house. Even though she was in town, I'd still dedicate the bulk of my time to getting my workouts in. Regardless of what was going on around me, I was on a mission, and I wasn't about to allow anything to cause me to lose focus on my athletic endeavors.

Show and Prove (1998-1999)

The next school year, when I started eleventh grade, I began to adopt a completely different persona than in previous years, since the person I was close to was now at FSU. No longer living in a family member's shadow was liberating for me. I felt I was able to unwind and be an authentic version of myself for a change. I also felt more prepared to play organized basketball than ever before.

In our Criminal Justice/Dual Enrollment Course, we would physically go to Miami-Dade Community College during the last period of the day for a class. It was exciting to be on a college campus, and it made me feel like we were VIPs. The difficult part was that I found it hard to truly appreciate the opportunity because I was fixated on other things besides academics.

Nothing else besides making the team concerned me, to be honest. On the contrary, I still made time to talk to an occasional female or two. My basketball skills had become considerably more polished than before. There was this uncanny confidence that I acquired from the many months of hard work I put in.

In school, I was still keeping my grades up and became even more sociable than in my freshman and sophomore years.

When basketball workouts started, I successfully made it through all the open gyms/runs and drills, as well as the dreaded "Hell Week." "Hell Week" was a six-day workout period where the coaching staff put together a full schedule of rigorous, yet absurd, physical activities that potential players had to complete in a timely fashion to be considered for the team.

That entire week, I pushed my body beyond its physical limits, and every time we had an activity, I would come in near the front of the pack. After "Hell Week" ended, we started practicing in the gym, and I performed really well. Coach J, the assistant coach, commended me on the great improvement that I'd shown. Even though I appreciated the compliment, I didn't dwell on it too much because I wanted to focus on performing to the best of my abilities. My jump shot was indeed more consistent, my defense was annoyingly aggressive, and my endurance/stamina was next level.

The day before tryouts, I was able to reflect and come to the realization that the time I spent working on my body and getting stronger helped me gain confidence I didn't have before. Then, unfortunately, after tryouts concluded, I was notified that I didn't make the cut once again. Not too long afterward, I went to Coach Bob's portable to find out why I didn't make the team. While standing directly in front of him, he tried to persuade me to go back to playing football, and I took that personally.

I resented the fact that he was trying to push me towards a sport I wasn't interested in. I felt like I put in the work, and I was playing my tail off, but it still didn't seem like it was enough. Coach stood by his decision to cut me and refused to reconsider the possibility of adding me to the team. However, he did explain to me how difficult the decision was for him not to put me on the team. He told me that he noticed how far I'd come athletically, but he didn't have enough roster space for me.

I left his portable that day, crushed; I couldn't believe what was going on. One day later, my close high school friends, P and Brian (who were on the basketball team), flat-out told me that Coach Bob didn't want me on the basketball team, plain and simple.

For a couple of weeks, I didn't speak to many people besides my immediate family members. As a matter of fact, I wasn't able to focus on anything based on the ordeal that recently transpired. That was when I said to myself, "Screw it, I'm never playing basketball again."

If the situation were a little different and I weren't at least a decent player who could've contributed to the team, I would've understood Coach Bob's decision better. I wouldn't have been upset whatsoever, but according to many players who were already on the team the previous year, they felt I was one of the better defensive players out there. I was so pissed off at Coach Bob and his assistant coach J for the rest of the year. Not only that, but I harbored a lot of ill-will for them, since I felt that their decision was possibly personal; Maybe they just didn't like me for whatever reason, or maybe it was something about the way I operated on the court?

The pain had gotten even worse to bear when the returning players started telling me they discovered that I didn't make the team because the coaches already knew who they wanted before tryouts, and even "Hell Week" began. So, I attempted to use that information as fuel in order to stage one final attempt for next year's team. I figured, "Hey, I've been through too much in my lifetime to let this petty situation get the best of me. I didn't give up when I was on the street, and I won't start now."

After the disappointment of not making the team set in, eventually, their season came and went almost at the blink of an eye. I went to a few games to support a few of my homeboys and to see the players the coaches chose to keep on the team instead of me.

Before I knew it, volleyball season had begun, and as usual, I
played well enough to earn Co-M.V.P. Surprisingly, our team
performed better than we'd expected, to the point that we actually
made it to the playoffs for the first time. We ended up playing a
top-ranked Miami Senior High team at Barbara Goleman High
School, and they demolished us, to put it lightly. Their jump serves
were so tremendous and overpowering that all we could do was
look at each other in amazement during the game. A few of my
teammates started arguing with each other out of frustration as our
team's confidence started to dwindle with the onslaught of points
the opposition continued to score.

We knew we were out of our league. Sporadically, we'd get
lucky enough to "dig" a few of their serves and eventually return
the ball to their side. One play that I remember in particular was
when they returned one of our weak attempts to spike the ball over
the net, with life-altering results. One of their front row blockers
smashed the ball back over to our side with so much force and
velocity that it caught me in the head before traveling out of
bounds. It was beyond embarrassing. My teammates started to
chuckle, but they also realized they could've been next, like lambs
to the slaughter. That was one of the featured plays where they
instilled the fear of God in us. It was at that point that reality sank
in that maybe, just maybe, we were "Inner city" good but not
"District Championship" good. We lost 21-1 in the first match and
21-3 in the second. They completely demoralized us, and the bus
ride back was so quiet and somber that it reminded me of a funeral
service.

All in all, the season was fun, and the bond that I was able to
build with my teammates was amazing. We had some pretty big
personalities on the team that year, which made the trips both to
and from the games highlight-worthy. From the jokes that were

cracked to the music we vibed to, it was one of the most memorable seasons ever. Regardless of whether we won or lost, we enjoyed competing against local teams with each other.

I also continued to visit my father on the weekends, and every other weekend we would go play basketball together. The next year (my senior year) would be an important year because it wasn't until then that I actually decided to apply to colleges. The older I got, the more I started to face the harsh reality that it was beyond time to start planning my future.

Someone Intriguing (1998)

There was this young lady, by the name of Kisha, who would draw some of my attention away from basketball and the stress associated with worrying about my future beyond high school. She was in my Algebra 2 class during my junior year, though she was only a sophomore. At the very beginning of the year, I used to converse with her now and then in class until one day, I suddenly gathered the courage to ask for her phone number.

I essentially tried a new approach. I didn't merely ask her, I told her, "What are you waiting on, you know you want to give me your number?" For some strange reason, something told me to try this approach when talking to this particular young lady because she had a feisty personality filled with sass and a bit of attitude. I don't know if it was instinct or my cousin's tutelage over the years that motivated me to be more assertive in this instance. Nevertheless, I just threw caution to the wind and went for it. The main question that crept into my mind was, "What's the worst that could happen?" Maybe I attempted this approach, hoping to catch her off guard and reduce the chances of her saying, "No" right away. This was the first time in my life that I attempted to pursue a girl so aggressively, and to be perfectly honest, it was an incredible adrenaline rush.

She crushed me a bit by laughing at me at first and telling me she had a boyfriend. Believe it or not, I was still able to get her phone number that day. We ended up talking on the phone for a couple of weeks, and we also became good friends. During our conversations, we discussed a plethora of topics, including family dynamics, our upbringing, and our future career goals. She would often tell me how badly her boyfriend was treating her and that she was getting ready to break up with him. Based on what my cousin often said to me about females from the area, I'd often take what this young lady told me about her boyfriend with a grain of salt, especially after hearing about some of the games many females were known for playing. Secretly, part of me was hoping and wishing that her current relationship went sour so I could put my bid in. I refused to say anything negative about her situation or her boyfriend because of the code my cousin taught me to follow: "Never hate on the next man nor their situation because there's always two to three sides to every story."

Then all of a sudden, I stopped seeing my friend in class. Come to find out, she stopped coming to school altogether. After a few failed attempts at calling her at home, I didn't hear from her again. Back in those days, we didn't have access to cellphones, and social media didn't exist. For a while, I was concerned for her personal well-being. The abrupt disappearance was crazy to me because I couldn't imagine just abruptly disappearing like that. I just know my conscience would've gotten the best of me if I were on the other end of the situation.

Summer League Debacle (1999)

Leading up to the end of my junior year of high school, I convinced myself to try out for my high school's summer league basketball team. I decided to try out for the team again after having a heart-to-heart with the coach. I thoroughly expressed my concerns with him about why I felt I was not getting a fair shake at making the team. Coach Bob then told me that all I had to do moving forward was play well during summer league and everything would take care of itself. Hesitantly, I took his word for it, even though I really felt he was full of it. I dapped him up and left his portable with a somewhat optimistic mindset.

There was no doubt on whether I was ready to ball out during summer league, so that was what I did. During my first actual game with the team, I scored eight points, collected three rebounds, and also blocked two shots off the bench. In my eyes, my debut was a success. I was very excited because that was the first time I actually felt full confidence about my abilities. The best part about my first game was that my father was in attendance. He was all smiles, and I know that he was proud of me, even though he didn't say so verbally. I believed I had proved to the coaching staff that I had great potential until game two came around the following week.

The next week was crazy. One of my fellow teammates, P, had car troubles, so I had to get my grandfather to pick him and a couple of my other teammates up so we could quickly get to the game. It didn't work out like we would've hoped, considering that we missed the entire first half of the game. To make matters worse, our team was down by twenty points when we finally arrived.

Coach Bob was pissed off; you could see it in his eyes. At halftime, when we finally arrived in the locker room, he cursed us out and called all ten of his seniors "Irresponsible." Then, after the game, during his post-game rant, he told all of us that we weren't on the team anymore, from that day forward. Everyone was speechless, and no one on the team wanted to make eye contact with each other or the coaches. At that point, to be completely transparent, I wasn't too worried about the whole ordeal because I felt that all of us pretty much deserved some disciplinary action, but there was no way he wasn't going to give us another chance.

A week later, I heard through the grapevine that all of my teammates were brought back for the start of the regular season, so I went to talk to Coach Bob to confirm the information. After school, as I was walking to my uncle's portable, I could hear basketballs bouncing in the gym. My inquisitive side was eager to get to the bottom of the situation at hand. I went to knock on the back door of the gymnasium. The previous year's starting point guard, Kee, opened the door and looked surprised to see me. He was sweating heavily, wearing a black jersey as if he were practicing or working out. I could tell he was in there with a few other people, but I didn't enter the gym to see who they were. I asked Kee, "Was Coach in there, and he said, "No, he isn't, and I was told not to let anyone in the gym!" I looked at him like he was Coach Bob's own personal messenger or something. I didn't make a big deal about it, and I calmly told him I needed to talk to Coach. I also asked him if he was back on the team.

He begrudgingly said, "Yeah!" I then asked him about Brian and P, and he said, "They're back too," but he also said that Coach mentioned that "they were going to pay for what they did during the summer, before they could play."

After that statement, I asked him, "Well, what about me? Why didn't he bring me back?"

His response was, "Coach said he has all the players that he wants to work with right now."

That was the most ridiculous thing that I had ever heard of in my entire life. That statement alone infuriated me, and I frantically went to his portable to look for him. I went into a rage. All I remember was tears running down my face while punching and kicking most of the objects that were around me at the time. When I finally caught up to him, he basically reiterated what Kee previously told me. I thanked him for taking the time to speak to me, shook his hand, and walked off from there. After a couple of weeks, I continued to play basketball whenever I had free time at a few local parks.

From that day forward, most of the players who played basketball around that time for our high school said it wasn't right that I wasn't on the team because I would have been, at the very least, a defensive asset. At first, the situation had me broken-hearted, but once again, I had to overcome the adversity and remain focused on my academic goals.

Abrupt Changes (1999)

To add insult to injury, something strange started occurring with my Great Grandma Carol. At 87 years old, she was as vibrant and spry as I could ever remember, but she began to call me by Lapoleon's name and occasionally forget who I was. My uncle told me, and the rest of the family, that Great Grandma Carol was experiencing the early stages of Alzheimer's. He would also tell me not to take offense at the things she would do or say because she wouldn't be able to help herself. She would often accuse me of stealing the weirdest things from her room on a daily basis.

One day, she accused me of stealing her undergarments; other days, I would be accused of stealing her money and her bible. It became a continuous cycle of events that enraged her, and I was the only person she would accuse.

My cousin's girlfriend, who was the mother of his newborn child, Tabitha, would soon move in with us and witness the spectacle for herself. She was a year younger than Lapolean and a year older than me. She and I got along well; come to find out, we shared similar upbringings in Miami. Tabitha and I were like brother and sister after a while, even though her and my cousin's relationship was always "rocky" at best.

Most of the time, when Grandma Carol would throw her fits, we'd all laugh it off, but whenever any of us would have guests over, it would get downright embarrassing. As time went by, she became increasingly accusatory. She even started telling anyone who would listen that I was taking things from her room and

117

purposely moving them around to make it seem as if she was going crazy.

Guess Whose Back (2000)

After Christmas Break, while in the hallway during school one day, a young lady approached me and stated,

"Kisha told me to tell you she said, Hi, and she also said to call her if you still have her number."

I angrily responded by saying, "Who? I know you ain't talking about Kisha Rollerson!"

The shock of the statement caught me off guard, considering that she ghosted me without an explanation last year. "It was as if she dropped off the face of the earth or something!"

After a few seconds of mindless pondering, I said, "Maybe she and I could have a conversation or two, so she can tell me why she disappeared on me."

Her friend caught an attitude and said, "Well, let me know something sooner rather than later because that girl really wants to talk to you."

I asked her, "Where she been?" and she said that information wasn't hers to tell.

Later that day, when I saw Kisha's friend again, I told her I needed Kisha's number, since I no longer had it. She reached into her jacket pocket and pulled out a sheet of paper with her number already written on it.

After handing me the paper, she said, "Make sure you call her asap, and I'll tell her to expect your call."

One of my friends from our school's marching band was apparently eavesdropping and overheard the conversation. He told me that Kisha stopped coming to school because she got pregnant by a guy in the band named Zay.

My first reaction was "Oh, this gotta be a joke!" I was furious. This was the same girl who used to sit on the phone with me, pouring her heart out about how her boyfriend wasn't faithful to her and how she was on the verge of breaking up with him. I just felt like I was being lied to the whole time we were talking on the phone. Even though my cousin always warned me, I doubt anything would've prepared me for this. This type of news was beyond comprehension. The curveball was also hearing that she had stopped entirely dealing with Zay after having the baby, for some reason. The word on the street was that she told her friends she realized I was good for her and that she should have just kept talking to me instead of continuing to deal with Zay off and on. Normally, I would have just blown the girl off like anyone else would've, but I felt that everybody makes mistakes, and they shouldn't be judged for making bad choices.

After careful deliberation, I eventually called her and she explained everything to me. She told me she found out she was a few months pregnant at a routine gynecologist visit that she went to with her mom. She said she was so devastated that she didn't communicate with anyone. Furthermore, she said that her mom and the guidance counselor decided that it was best for her to enroll at a school for expectant mothers immediately. She stated that she knew that she should've communicated with me, but she was afraid of what I would've thought of her. She didn't want to be judged, and she didn't know if I'd believe her account of what happened. While she was talking, I made it seem like I believed her story (Thank God there was no FaceTime back in those days), although, in actuality, I didn't. I would hit her with the classic words and phrases of, "Yeah?" "Really?" "Wow, that's crazy!" Those were the go-to words we used back then, when we were listening but not truly listening at the same time. When she was done talking, I explained to her how I felt when she seemingly disappeared off the face of the earth. She immediately said that she understood things from my perspective, and we agreed to start over from scratch.

At first, it was strange talking to her after not speaking with her since the beginning of the previous school year. I asked her about the pregnancy, and she told me that she had recently had the baby and that she and the ex were co-parenting. According to Kisha, she and her baby's father agreed that having a relationship together wasn't the best thing for them. With that established, I decided to let bygones be bygones and try to pick up where we left off with the friendship we started to develop last year. We would speak on the phone often, from that point.

* * *

Striving for the Finish line

Toward the latter part of my senior year of high school, I maintained a 3.47 grade point average, and I was in the top 15% of my graduating class. Additionally, I was in the process of earning up to 24 college credits in the Dual Enrollment Program, thanks to my favorite teacher, Mr. Henry.

All the accomplishments were fine and dandy, though the most important issue around that time was getting at least an 850 on the SATs or at least a 21 on the ACTs. Those were the qualifying scores I needed to be accepted into college based on my current

121

grade point average. Without either one of those scores, all the accolades would have been for nothing. The first time I took the SAT, I didn't study much, and I was still able to receive a score of 830. Before the second time I took the test, I studied extensively, and there were many nights when I would barely sleep due to all-night review sessions. Unfortunately, no matter how much I studied, I still scored a disappointing 820. I decided that was the last time I would take that particular test because I felt I had a better chance of passing the ACT. I actually studied for the ACT a little, and when I took it, I scored a 19. So, I told myself, "Well, combined these scores should be good enough for college, considering that I have a 3.47 grade point average.

Afterward, I submitted my admissions application to Florida Atlantic University to explore other ways to get accepted. I was sure I would be accepted since my grades were better than average. I had also accumulated over 70 hours of community service for volunteering at a local elementary school. I was able to earn the hours by tutoring troubled kids in math and social studies at Brentwood Elementary. I even submitted multiple letters of recommendation, so my character would not have come into question.

While waiting for a response from the university, I worked on a project to help EJ achieve a passing score on the SAT. Since he had become a star running back at our high school, he only needed a qualifying score to be accepted into FAU as well. It seemed like we both had a somewhat similar problem, even though EJ was offered a full athletic scholarship to play football at FAU. All he had to do was get at least an 850 on his SATs, and he would be set to go. He came to me for help because, after the first time he took the test, he received a 650 without studying. After a long week of meeting with him every day at a local library, I taught him which questions to answer and which to avoid. When it came time to retake the test, he was able to earn a 900. We both were ecstatic because neither of us expected such a huge jump from his previous score to the second time he took the test.

The following week, I received a notice in the mail from FAU. Before opening the letter, I wasn't hopeful. I figured it was a rejection letter. After the disappointing situations I've gone through over the years, I was used to the constant letdowns from other people's bad decisions. When I opened the notice, it stated that I needed to submit a letter explaining to the admissions board why my test score (on the math portion of the SAT) didn't align with my GPA. In a little less than 48 hours, I did it! I typed a five to six-page essay explaining to the university's admissions board that, due to a troubled childhood, I was not able to learn most of the material that average children around my age were typically taught in elementary and middle school. Then I continued by telling the admissions board that I've never used my childhood upbringing as an excuse for anything. As a result, I'd adapt rather than fold under pressure. I also mentioned how I went to the library every day to catch up on the materials I wasn't fortunate enough to learn when I was younger. Once I sent the letter, all I could do was wait.

***

Blind Prom Date

In the meantime, one of my friends named Brian called me one evening and asked if I was planning on going to the prom and, if so, whether I had a date yet.

My response was, "I hadn't asked anyone yet, and quite honestly, I've been more concerned with trying to get accepted into college."

He told me that his girl's best friend needed a date.

I asked him, "What's the catch?"

He stated that his girl would only go to the prom if her friend could come too, but he would need to find a date for her since they didn't attend our school.

At first, I was led to think he was kidding, so in an attempt to call his bluff, I said, "Yeah, why not?"

Little did I know, he immediately put me on a three-way call with his girl, Linda, and her friend, Crystal. I was shocked to hear that the situation was real, and she was ok with the idea of going on a blind prom date with me. We asked each other a million and one questions. Then we both agreed that we would exchange numbers and continue to get to know each other. We talked for a couple of weeks, and things were so cool that we put our plan to wear matching outfits to the prom in motion. The plan was for Brian to have his family rent a car for him, and we would ride together to the prom (with our dates, of course).

After getting to know Crystal a bit, through our various telephone conversations, she seemed pretty cool. The strangest thing was that she always used to ask me if I knew certain guys who also attended my high school. Things got even weirder when she asked me about guys who graduated a year or so before I did. She didn't elaborate too much when I asked her why she was asking me about other guys. I didn't make an issue out of it since my intentions weren't to get into a relationship with her or anything. I should've known those were red flags at the time, even though I was focused on everything else happening in my life except the prom.

A couple of weeks later, the day before prom, to be exact, Uncle Stetson handed me a letter that was sent from FAU. It must've arrived in the mail that same day, judging by the way he handed it to me. I think he was just as excited as I was to find out what the admissions board decided. I was too nervous to open it right away. After a minute or two of stalling, I finally opened the letter that stated I was conditionally accepted for the Fall semester. That was one of the most gratifying moments in my life. My uncle congratulated me and told me that he was proud. I immediately called my dad, and he congratulated me as well. Everyone I called to share the wonderful news with was elated that I was finally accepted into college.

Once my Federal Application for Student Aid was fully processed by the state of Florida, I received a ton of financial aid and Pell Grant funds that covered my room and board, tuition, and other expenses (as long as I kept my grades up and I was enrolled as a full-time student).

Senior Prank (2000)

Now that my future was set, it was time to have a little fun. I called EJ on a Thursday night and told him that we were going to prank the entire school by pretending to fight after school on Friday. He laughed at the idea, but swiftly agreed. We both agreed to go to school in the morning, visibly upset, so our friends, teammates, or associates would be tempted to ask us what was wrong. From there, we would be able to stoke the flames of controversy to draw attention to our make-believe beef. The goal was to get as many of our schoolmates as possible to come to the student parking lot area to watch our fake fight.

We put our devious plan in play as soon as we arrived at school. I manufactured a scowl that put my peers on notice that I was visibly upset about something. As I walked through the hallway, some of them asked me whether or not everything was alright.

Initially, I'd respond with, "No, everything ain't alright," but as the morning progressed, I provided more details about my "make-shift" situation.

I intentionally told people who I knew couldn't hold water specific details about what was troubling me.

I'd go as far as saying, "He tried me, bro, I'm about to split him after school in the parking lot!"

Not only would I say it, but I'd add aggressive hand gestures to make the statement more believable. I would have to do my best to really sell it, since everyone knew that we were close friends. Right before lunch, I even made a big scene in the hallway when I was talking about what led up to the beef that EJ and I had. The more students who crowded around me, the more they believed that he and I really were going to fight at the end of the day.

One of my former teammates from the football team, named "Dank," came up to me and said, "Bro what the hell you and 'Swole' got going on? Y'all really wanna fight each other? What happened?"

The reason they called EJ "Swole" was that, physically, he was the pure definition of muscle-bound for his age. At eighteen, he intimidated many of our peers because he was a beast in the weight room as well as on the football field. No one wanted any smoke with EJ, since many of our classmates felt he had a few screws loose. Thank God, I had actually gotten to know him. Therefore, I knew better than most. EJ was a good dude, just misunderstood, like many of us. He didn't tolerate anyone mistaking his kindness for weakness.

Later, at the end of the day, after the final bell, as I stepped out of class, I noticed that the hallways were eerily emptier than usual. As I approached the door leading to the student parking lot, a group of students was gathered around it. There was a lot of ranting and raving going on, and all I could hear next was, "Oh, there he go! It's about to go down, Swole outside waiting on him!" It was at that point that I knew that EJ and I did a terrific job of selling this fake fight. Even though we weren't really going to fight, I was still a bit on edge because so many students lingered after school to see it happen.

Normally, most of the student body would quickly exit the campus to go home or hang out somewhere. Today, though, I knew it would be different. People were expecting a spectacle immediately after school since the word had gotten out.

Once I made it to the door, one of my classmates approached me and said, "Here, bro, you might need this!"

He tried to give me a piece of 2x4 that he found over by the portables.

I looked at him with an arrogant look on my face and told him, "Bro, I don't need that. You might want to give that to him instead of me!"

He responded by saying, "Oh, you must have fire on you, ain't no way in Hell you have a chance against him!"

As he was speaking, I took my bookbag and violently flung it on the pavement. I was seemingly ready to brawl. I could hear our principal, Mrs. Henry, on her bullhorn, telling everyone to go home, on the far side of the student parking lot.

I was hesitant to proceed because Mrs. Henry, or "Big Bird" as some of us nicknamed her, was a rather intimidating character herself. She was at least 6'4 and as mean as a whip. She was the wrong one to play with, and she had a reputation for going toe to toe with anyone who wanted to cause trouble on her campus. After a few minutes, she left the student parking lot and returned to the building.

When the coast was clear, I scanned the parking lot, piercing through the massive crowd, looking for EJ, and we finally spotted each other. As soon as our eyes connected, I could tell that he was trying to resist the urge to smile. From there, we improvised, and we aggressively charged toward each other, cursing and carrying on. I could feel that all eyes were focused on us, and chants were radiating through the crowd of "Fight, fight, fight!" When EJ and I got within striking distance of each other, we faked swinging motions, hugged each other, and laughed hysterically.

Simultaneously, we turned around, laughed, and pointed at everyone who came out to witness the fight, as we yelled, "Sike, got y'all stupid ass!"

It was hilarious to us, but most of the spectators were furious.

I heard "Dank" say, "I should've known y'all were full of crap! Y'all ain't sh**!"

After a few minutes, everyone laughed off the chaotic scene and returned to their normal after-school routines. It was definitely one of the best memories from my time in high school.

Unpleasant Surprise (May 2000)

On the day of prom, I was ready to go and extremely nervous at the same time. Leading up to that day, I had only seen Crystal once, when I met up with her to get a color sample for the dress she was having customized (We wanted to ensure that my tuxedo matched her dress). The plan was for Brian to pick me up first and then ride over to each of our date's houses to pick them up. As we were picking them up, we presented our respective dates with corsages, and we essentially "rolled out the red carpet" for them. My tux and Crystal's dress were both crème-colored, and when we arrived at the Fontainebleau Restaurant and Resort, we looked like a million bucks.

We all strolled into the establishment with the biggest grins on our faces. As we all sat down together, we greeted many of our friends as if we hadn't seen them in a long time. That's when things started to take a turn for the worse.

P approached me with a surprised look on his face, chuckled, and asked, "Yo Baybay, you brought Crystal?"

With a perplexed look on my face, I said, "Yeah, why?"

He responded with, "Boy, you don't know about Crystal?"

He told me to ask the boys who were currently there about her. To make a long story short, after talking to four other male classmates at the venue, they all said they've either dealt with her in some capacity or had a homeboy who has. I was so ashamed and embarrassed after finding out that my blind date was known around town for the wrong reasons, to say the least. I knew I'd have to keep my poker face on to avoid making her feel some way all of a sudden.

Moving forward, I played things off the entire time while we were there, but behind the scenes, I had already pulled Brian aside to advise him that we should drop our dates off at home once we left. When he asked me why, I told him what everyone was telling me, and he apologized to me for setting me up with someone with a large body count. He agreed to drop them off at home after leaving the venue. Brian told me that he'll make an excuse so they won't ask a bunch of questions while dropping them off. He said he'll circle back and hang out with Linda later that night. I truly appreciated his cooperation, knowing that he didn't have to agree to do so.

After dropping the young ladies off, we linked up with the rest of our homeboys and hung out for the rest of the night. When a few guys asked me why I didn't take advantage of the fact that Crystal was "known" around town, I responded by letting them know that I wasn't into that type.

For the duration of the night, we raced the rental cars and "Dined and Ditched" at the local Denny's restaurant that we all occasionally frequented. Once I was dropped off at home, I called Kisha and we talked about how my evening went. She did (deservedly so) give me a hard time about going to the prom with Crystal, and she couldn't believe we dropped her and Linda off immediately afterward. To get my point across, I called Brian on a three-way call to verify what transpired, even though she said that I "didn't need to do all of that."

Graduation Present (2000)

The week before my high school graduation, my dad told me that my mom and sister were flying down to attend. He also said that all of us would be spending that weekend together and that I would need to make sure that I didn't have any plans. I knew what he was alluding to, indirectly telling me to get my nose out of "that girl's" rear-end and come up for air for a change. He did have a point; I was spending a lot of time either on the phone or visiting Kisha in person.

One interesting tidbit he shared with me was that he was planning to rent a car so Grace and I could hang out. He wanted to give us the chance to get up and go whenever we wanted while they were in town. I guess he realized one of the hardest things to do as a teenager was finding people to bum rides from while trying to get around. The hotel we stayed in when my mom and my sister arrived was beautiful. It was an all-inclusive resort near Miami Beach. We really had a nice time together, and my parents told me that they had another surprise graduation present.

After the graduation ceremony was over, they would unveil the big surprise. Many of my father's side of the family attended my graduation, and we took many pictures to celebrate. It was a great day, and I appreciated all the kind words that everyone had for me. Walking across the stage to commemorate my graduation was a mere formality that I didn't care for too much. I felt that if it weren't for wanting to please Granny and my aunts, I probably wouldn't have walked across the stage. I was satisfied with getting my diploma and starting a new chapter in my life, to be honest. Not only that, but I wasn't too big on all the hoopla associated with the ceremony, either. Mentally, I was already preparing myself for college.

After walking across the stage and taking all the family photos, my mom and dad told me they managed to rekindle their relationship. They, along with my sister, were moving to Miami after Grace graduated from high school the following year. I was beyond dumbfounded and highly confused. They could see the concern all over my face, so my dad said that he and my mom have been speaking over the phone every day. He even traveled back and forth from Florida to Texas during the holidays. He also included that he was in the process of purchasing a 2-bedroom apartment in Miami Lakes.

Many different thoughts and emotions went through my head. The emotions that weighed heavily on my heart were anger and frustration. Even though I smiled and told my dad how excited I was to hear the shocking news, I couldn't help but replay all the turmoil that he and I experienced since the day my mom and sister left South Florida. A part of me felt that if they had remained together in the first place, instead of splitting, things more than likely wouldn't have spiraled out of control as much as they did. Maybe I wouldn't have spent all those years on the street while experiencing the type of torture that could destroy a child mentally, physically, and emotionally.

After graduation, the reality of my dwindling time in the Dade and Broward County areas was rapidly approaching. For another surprise graduation present, my dad took me to a Cingular Wireless Store and bought me a cellphone. Once I got the phone in my hand, I felt like no one could tell me anything. It was a black-on-black, T18LX Sony Ericsson flip phone. The first five contacts that I put in it were my dad, my uncle, Granny, Lapolean, and

Kisha. Speaking of Kisha, the number of conversations with her increased rapidly.

Very soon after receiving an invitation, I began taking trips over to her house to visit and catch up. I had the privilege to meet her mother, brothers, and her baby boy. Everything was so cool between the two of us that we started spending the majority of our free time together, especially when her baby daddy had their son. The two of us had fallen for each other so fast that we didn't focus too much on the fact that I was set to go off to college in August.

Around that time, many of my friends, including some family members, were telling me I shouldn't have gotten involved with her since she had just had a baby with someone she wasn't in a committed relationship with. Although they all had valid points, I wouldn't listen because I was infatuated with her. Therefore, I didn't want to hear anything negative about who I believed was the love of my life at that time.

I'd eventually introduce her to my dad and Granny, as well as some of my other family members. I even had her come to Granny's house during one of our family reunion events that summer. Granny and Grandpa Theodore bragged to the entire fam' once they found out I was accepted into FAU.

Everyone at the event expressed their happiness for me. The peculiar thing about it was that my grandmother and Grandpa Theodore went from telling their associates around town that I'd end up like my father years ago to telling people that I'd be the next Judge Joe Brown. They didn't know that I was aware of the hurtful things they used to say to people when my dad and I were down on our luck. I kept my mouth shut and used it as motivation to persevere, even when the obstacles in front of me seemed too heavy to bear. Toward the end of that evening, before Kisha went home, she and I shared our first passionate kiss (away from the adults, of course). From that day forward, I was hooked like a fox in a hen house. As my time in town started winding down, I told her how concerned I was about going off to school while trying to maintain a long-distance relationship. She tried to ease my mind by telling me not to worry and "We'll make it work." Unfortunately, the next few months went by as fast as Usain Bolt at the Olympics.

Death of a Former Teammate (2000)

That same summer, right before I left for college, I got a call from Brian saying, "BayBay, Ray is in the hospital, he has meningitis."

I felt numb all over because he had a larger-than-life personality, and he was also a former teammate of ours. He was the center for our high school's basketball team, and he also played on the volleyball team with us. Ray, aka "Disco Stick," was about 6'9" and always fun to be around. He had the brightest personality, and he was the life of the party all the time. Those were some of the reasons why it was so hard to picture him in a hospital bed, suffering.

I was told he was found in his bed, bleeding from his mouth, eyes, and ears, but he was still alive. The word was that he was being quarantined and treated at a local hospital. After speaking with my uncle about the ordeal, we decided we would go try to see him, and then, before we could leave, Brian called me back and told me Ray died. An uneasy numbness consumed my entire body. I dropped the receiver of the house phone on the ground and sobbed uncontrollably.

The next several hours were a complete blur. All I could think about was the good times around our high school campus and at the various volleyball games we played in together. It was truly a tough pill to swallow. On our way to his wake, I remember the local radio station, 99-Jamz, ironically playing DRS's old hit single called "Gangsta Lean." The song was so sad, and I couldn't hold back the tears as I continued to reminisce. Unfortunately, I could not bring myself to go to his funeral because the pain of losing a friend and a teammate was too much to bear.

Almost Lost It All (2000)

After Ray died, Zo, P, Brian, and I decided to hang out before we all went our separate ways. Zo, who was one year older than us, was in town from college. We would go out to Lake Shore and the outside court at Broward Community College to play pickup basketball games throughout the week. The games were fun, intense at times, and memorable.

One night, we decided to go out and get into some trouble in the community. We put our money together to purchase cartons of eggs. Each of us had a few dollars, but we needed a little more to acquire the amount of artillery that would leave a mark. Zo drove us to the Overtown area, where his mom lived, to ask her for a contribution. He and his mom had a rather complex relationship. They kept it real with one another at all times, so he decided to tell her what he really needed the money for. She reluctantly gave him a few dollars, but with a stern warning not to get into trouble because she wouldn't bail him out if he got caught.

After acquiring more than enough money to get what we needed, we went to the local Winn-Dixie to buy the eggs. We took turns riding up and down various streets in Overtown and Liberty City, throwing eggs at unsuspecting victims. I was the initiator of the events, but we all played our parts well. We were indeed on "Demon Time." At the time, it seemed fun to hit random people we didn't know. Looking back, it was cruel and unusual, but we enjoyed ourselves in the heat of the moment.

After that night, we still had a few dollars left over, so P, Zo, and I decided to use the last bit of cash to buy a crate full of eggs for another repeat performance. Zo picked all of us up, and we headed back down to 69th Street and 27th Avenue. We were more animated this particular night. We had just finished playing pickup basketball, and our adrenaline was already pumping well before engaging in the dastardly deeds.

Not only that, but we were absolutely beaming at people on bus stops, homeless men, and kids walking down the street. As we were starting to run low on inventory, I spotted a middle-aged Spanish guy on an oversized ladder painting a building. I had two eggs left, and I was determined to hang out the window and catch the guy while he was suspended in the air. As I threw the eggs and inadvertently missed him, I pulled the egg crate from the back seat out of frustration and threw it at the guy unsuccessfully as well. As soon as I let the bulky black egg crate loose from my hand and launched it towards the guy on the ladder, I could see red and blue lights flashing directly behind us.

That's right, it was a police car. One of the officers in the vehicle utilized his public announcement system to tell us to "Pull over immediately!" All of us were terrified. After getting pulled over, the two officers who approached with caution told all of us to get out of the car and sit on the curb. While we were there, another cop car pulled up. They asked Zo for consent to search the vehicle, and he agreed. The officers decided to put all of us in handcuffs and shoved us in the back of the patrol cars while they ran all of our licenses and searched the vehicles for any illegal paraphernalia. We were all taller than your average young man. Zo was 6'4", 250+, P was 5'11", 220+, and I was 6'2 ", 165. We were in there, visibly shaken because we all had so much at stake. I kept thinking out loud, "Man, I think I just ruined my chance at going to college!"

139

The officers kept us in the backseat of their patrol car for at least forty-five minutes, though it felt like an eternity. To make matters worse, I mistakenly sat on the cuffs, which caused them to tighten and dig into my wrists. It was some of the most excruciating pain that I'd felt in a while.

Every time they came to the car to talk to us, we would unsuccessfully attempt to plead our cases on why they should let us go with a warning. Eventually, the officer's supervisor came out, spoke to us, and said that the Spanish guy on the ladder didn't want to press charges. We would be released; the only catch was that P would be transported to the county jail for processing because he had an open bench warrant for missing a court date (traffic violation).

Once we were out of the handcuffs and the officers went to take our homeboy to jail, we knew we had to find a way to get him out. We eventually found out we would need $500 to get P out. We called everyone we knew, as well as P's family. Zo even called his mom, but she quickly hung up the phone when she was told about the trouble we got into.

Suddenly, he remembered that P had a lady friend who worked at a McDonald's in Miramar. We decided to go to the young lady's job, hoping she was actually at work at the time and would be willing to help bond him out. When we arrived, we realized we were lucky she was indeed working, and she told us she'd help. All we had to do was wait for her shift to end so we could drive her to an ATM. When we reached Turner Guilford Knight Correctional Center, we were able to get P bonded out of jail. We were all relieved too because things could've gone worse that night, and I think we learned our lesson.

Off to College (2000)

A week or so before the first semester of class started, my dad took me up to FAU to drop me off. When we arrived at the school's gymnasium to get the necessary documentation and dorm room keys, there were many freshmen in the parking lot. During the orientation portion of the presentation, I couldn't believe I was actually about to start college. It seemed surreal.

When I received the room keys and went to the Timucua Building, I was ecstatic. The suite was a decent size for four people. Inside, there were two rooms connected, with a bathroom in the middle. In each room, there were two twin-sized beds located on opposite sides. Each room contained two mini refrigerators with microwaves attached to the top. I knew for me, the biggest adjustment would be having a roommate who wasn't a family member. The opportunity to be on my own while earning a college degree overshadowed any potential challenges that I faced.

A little later that day, my friend EJ came over to check my room out and to say, "What's up?" to my dad. Since EJ was there on a football scholarship, he didn't live in the dorms. He resided in the student apartments, which were located on the opposite side of the campus. When I walked with him to the apartments to check out his room, it seemed like a huge upgrade from the dorms I lived in.

For the first few weeks, it was obviously an adjustment period. I started to make a few friends that I wouldn't have back home in Miami. Most of the time, if you attended a particular high school,

141

kids didn't really look to befriend kids from other schools, unless you grew up in the same neighborhood over the years.

***

Friends

In college, I learned pretty quickly that most people from Miami gravitated to each other. Coming from the same city was unquestionably a strong common denominator that led to solid relationships being established right away. I also discovered that there were some quality people from other parts of the state as well, but it would take me a little longer to let my guard down for them.

While getting acquainted with the wide variety of people at FAU, one of the first out-of-towners that I met was Joe. We met while working out in the school's weight room. While conversing, I discovered that he was a former high school basketball player from the Orlando, Florida area. He also told me that he was an "Invited walk-on" for the FAU's basketball team, and tryouts were going to be held sometime in October. He would eventually introduce me to someone he met a day or two ago, named Dee.

Dee was also an "Invited walk-on" basketball player from Orlando, Florida. Since I was working out and hooping with them almost every day, I decided to try out as well when the time came. I figured it wouldn't hurt to see how I stacked up against the other walk-ons, although I could immediately tell that Dee and Joe were on a different level, skill-wise. Joe was a terrific ball handler who thrived on embarrassing his opposition. His skill set reminded me of some of the players from the Harlem Globetrotters. Dee, on the other hand, was more of a no-nonsense type of hooper who wanted to dominate anyone who dared to get in his way. He wasn't as flashy as Joe, but he was more physical and consistent. He was more of a three-level scorer who had an awesome mid-range jumper. He wouldn't hesitate (unless he wanted to) to take a defender straight to the hoop with either hand. When tryouts for the basketball team came and went, both Dee and Joe made the team, and my efforts during tryouts weren't enough to make it beyond the first cut.

Dee and I would end up hanging out more often because we shared many common interests. Joe and I's relationship went from the occasional friendly banter to oil and water. After a while, every time we'd be around each other, people could tell there was some weird tension between us. It almost seemed competitive in nature, for some reason or another. There were things that I witnessed Joe engage in that I didn't necessarily agree with, from trying to backdoor his friends by flirting with their girls behind their backs to gossiping and talking about his so-called friends when they weren't around. Don't get me wrong, we all had our faults and shortcomings, but some things were just inexcusable coming from where I came from. I was always big on loyalty, and when I would notice someone around me who wasn't loyal, I'd cut them off with the quickness.

Love Interest Back Home (2000)

I would still talk to Kisha every day, even though I was in Boca Raton and she was back at Carol City, finishing up her senior year. I would even catch the Tri-Rail to Miami to see her every other weekend. After I'd get off the Tri-Rail, I would often call different people to pick me up and drop me off at her mother's house to spend quality time with her. It was a lot, but I felt she was worth it.

After a few months, I stopped hearing from her as frequently as I'd grown accustomed to. The biweekly visits I made rapidly decreased because I could no longer confirm when she would be free to make adequate travel arrangements. To avoid constantly overthinking the situation, I tried to keep myself occupied with my coursework and other campus activities. I didn't even consider that she was potentially ghosting me again. Then, before I knew it, after a few weeks had gone by, I noticed that I wasn't hearing from her at all. I had no idea what was taking place with our relationship, and it started taking a toll on my ability to focus academically.

Eventually, she would call me one evening, out of the blue, and let me know that we needed to talk. She had this monotone pitch in her voice that led me to believe that something was going on, so I braced myself for what was to come.

The following few words out of her mouth were, "I can't do this anymore."

Then I responded with, "Do what anymore?"

She said, "Us."

My heart dropped immediately, and my only response was, "Why not?"

She continued by saying that she didn't feel like she and I were together anymore. She also said that she couldn't deal with feeling locked down and didn't want me to feel the same way while I was away at school.

My next response was, "Well damn, do you at least still love me?"

Her answer was "Yes," but I felt that was far from the truth because if she truly still loved me, she would have found a better way to break up with me than doing it over the phone.

From that point on, I'd start to travel down a dark path that consisted of weeks of rendezvous with a variety of different young ladies from around campus, partying/clubbing, physical altercations at on-campus events, and occasional drinking, to name a few. Most of the aforementioned activities were done when I was with the guys I gravitated toward when I first arrived on campus. Although I never smoked, I even unsuccessfully tried my hand at selling weed I got from one of my homeboys from Miami. I also got into the hobby of writing rap songs, which I was decent at. I would grab free beats from online websites and create lyrics similar to those I'd grown up listening to.

***

Academically, things were so bad after my second semester that I received a letter from the university stating I was placed on academic probation. I realized I was merely going through the motions with my coursework. I totally lost sight of who I was and all the hard work it took for me to get here. From that moment on, I knew I would have to focus more on my studies than on acting out of character. Everywhere I went on campus, the name "Baybay" would come up for partaking in so much foolishness. My alter ego began to take on a life of its own. I'd start to divert a little more attention to getting my coursework completed during the day, but at night, I turned into "Baybay" and became the life of the party everywhere I went. The attention was like a drug, and I couldn't get enough of it. When my freshman year ended, I successfully made it through, and I was no longer on academic probation.

Summer Work (2001)

Finding a summer job was tough at first, especially since I had to rely on public transportation to get to and from potential job interviews. When my aunt heard that I was looking for work, she called me and told me that her neighbor from across the street owned a construction company named Hillard Incorporated. She also told me that I should come over so I can talk to him.

The next day, I asked my uncle if he could take me to Auntie Teresa's house, and he agreed to do so as soon as he was done changing the oil in his car. After arriving at her house, she told me to head across the street, where Mr. Hillard was awaiting my arrival. When I got there, I was greeted warmly by his wife, Debbie. She was so nice and welcoming. She offered me a blueberry muffin and a cold glass of water, which I politely declined. It was bad enough that I was coming over here to ask for a job opportunity. I didn't want to give the appearance of being greedy. It was a gesture I wasn't accustomed to, outside of family.

After a quick conversation and an inquiry into whether I had my driver's license, Mr. Hillard offered me a part-time job as a parts manager for his company. Coincidentally, his company was currently working on expanding the runways at Miami International Airport. My role would consist of driving one of the company's pickup trucks around the city while picking up and delivering construction parts to various construction sites near and around the airport. I was so excited and scared at the same time. I'd never been hired by the owner of a company before, and I didn't want to let Mr. Hillard or my aunt down by doing a less-than-satisfactory job. There were still quite a few logistics to figure out before I would start working. The first issue would be finding transportation to and from work. The second issue consisted of finding out what type of car I wanted and the amount of money I would have to save up to buy it.

After telling him about my goal, my dad told me that he would help me search for a car once I was able to save anywhere from $1,000 to $2,000, before the end of the summer. He also advised me to "Man up" and take the city bus to and from the job site throughout the week. For the first couple of weeks, my dad would also give me enough money to get back and forth on my own, until I received my first paycheck. I appreciated the assistance, and I knew that if I really wanted the car that I desired, I was going to have to grin and bear whatever adversity came my way. My uncle would ask me if I needed anything, and I would tell him no, since I felt that he'd already helped enough by providing me with what I really needed for years, which was a stable home and the opportunity to reach my full potential. For that, I was forever indebted to him for the rest of my life.

The first couple of days, my main objective as far as the summer job was concerned was to complete the required Airfield Operations Area Driver Training Program. The training was administered by Miami-Dade County's Aviation Department, and it was pretty cool. There were videos, interactive components, and discussions throughout the session. It was easy to see that I was by far the youngest person there. The older, more experienced men that I took the training with all looked at me with amazement, due to the massive age gap between them and me. On June 14th, my training was complete, and I was officially certified to drive at the Airport. I immediately realized that I was one step closer to earning the funds to get my own car. Upon completion of the course, I was given a bright-colored work vest, a hard hat suitable for construction, an ID badge with my name and face on it, as well as a walkie-talkie.

During the first week on the job, I would drive around with one of the full-time employees, named Steve, until I became comfortable driving one of the company trucks alone. Every day that summer, my routine consisted of walking to Lake Lucerne from my uncle's house to catch multiple city buses. From there, I'd get transfer tickets to ride the Tri-Rail to the worksite that was just outside the airport (the distance between my uncle's house and the airport was 20 miles). After working for hours, I'd catch the Tri-Rail and the city buses back to Lake Lucerne in order to walk back to my uncle's house in Miramar.

Initially, the walk felt embarrassing due to all the gear that I had on, but after a few days, I grew accustomed to it. At work, when I began to drive one of the company trucks around town, I felt like I was an official part of the Hillard crew, and I appreciated the fact that I was trusted with such a great responsibility.

Car Hunting (2001)

In mid-July, after saving just about $1,500, my dad took me to a few used car lots to get a feel for what type of vehicle I wanted. Everywhere we went, it seemed like Chevy Impalas continuously caught my eye. The problem was that they were out of my price range. We decided to go to one more car lot in Pembroke Pines. As we pulled up to the establishment, there was a white 1991 Chevy Caprice Classic that I was quickly drawn to.

When we parked and got out of the car, the salesman approached us, wanting to chit-chat and make small talk. I urgently cut him off and asked, "How much for the Chevy Caprice over there?" The salesman looked over at the car I pointed to and said, "$2,000," depending on whether we were financing or purchasing with cash. As soon as I got ready to tell him how much cash I had, my dad stopped me dead in my tracks before I could continue.

He pulled me to the side and said, "Let me handle this!" In less than a second, my dad took on an assertiveness that I hadn't seen in a while. He told the guy that we'd like to check the car out and test drive it, if possible. The salesman obliged, and we all got into the car after he obtained the keys from his office.

As soon as we opened the doors of the pristine Chevy, I quickly noticed that the interior was impressively clean and all burgundy. When I stuck the key in the ignition, something told me at that very moment that I had to get this car. As I pulled out of the parking lot and made a right onto the main street, it felt as if I was steering a chariot. The ride was so smooth and satisfying, I was truly at a loss for words. When the salesman asked how we felt about the car so far, my dad interrupted and said, "It's ok, the suspension made noise when we first got into the car." I looked at my dad like he had lost his mind. I couldn't help but think to myself, "Has this dude relapsed and started smoking crack again?" Little did I know he was using some of the tricks that he had up his sleeves to get the overall price of the car down even lower than what it already was.

After he finished using his gift of gab, we managed to get the car for a little over twelve hundred dollars after taxes and fees. Nevertheless, I was so excited to have my own car finally, but I knew my first order of business was to get a stereo system installed when I received my next paycheck.

The Accident (2001)

The following week went by faster than the previous weeks. Maybe that was the case since I'd been driving to and from work instead of taking public transportation. Thank God, my uncle was able to rig the factory radio up in my car so I could listen to 99 Jamz and Power 96. I couldn't wait to get paid the following week so I could buy a new Kenwood CD player with a detachable face. I had my eyes on one ever since I went browsing for one at a local Brands Mart.

That Friday was exceptionally hot, so while at work, I decided to drive the company truck with the windows down and the air conditioner on full blast. During lunchtime, as I was returning to the worksite from picking up a package, there was a bright orange Asplundh truck on the side of the road. Around the truck, there were a bunch of orange cones aligned along its side. I assumed the cones were used to signify that some work was taking place.

As I approached the part of the road where the truck was parked, I rapidly slowed down. Suddenly, a short, middle-aged Haitian guy with a construction vest and a hard hat on, casually stepped into the street. When he came out beyond the orange cones, the mirror on the passenger side of the truck I was driving viciously smacked him on the head. I pulled over and jumped out to check on him as soon as the accident occurred. As I ran to the guy's aid, I asked if he was alright.

He replied, "Oww my head," while holding his head with two hands. The guy had a strong accent, and he started yelling things in Haitian-Creole that I couldn't understand. I quickly took out my cellphone and called 911 to get help, just in case he was in dire need of medical attention. Afterward, I called my supervisor to let him know what transpired and where it occurred. Ironically, the ambulance, the police, and my supervisor basically arrived at the same time. I was so nervous because I assumed I'd end up going to jail while losing my job in the process.

Fortunately, when the officer who interviewed me discovered that the guy who was struck stepped out into the road (beyond the orange cones), his actions were considered negligent, and he was deemed responsible for the incident. Before they loaded the guy into the ambulance, he received a citation from the officer who had previously interviewed me. The outcome shocked me, and I felt bad for the guy because he was just working, minding his business, and now he's on his way to the hospital, received a ticket, and will probably miss valuable time off work.

After thinking about what could've happened, I considered the situation as, "Another bullet dodged." My supervisor told me not to worry about the accident because it was obvious that there was nothing that I could've done differently, since I wasn't at fault. Considering that I was off the hook legally, I didn't hesitate to share the details of what transpired that day with my family. Some of them were concerned, while others giggled or laughed hysterically once they found out the guy that I hit was ok. Needless to say, I became the butt of many jokes during family get-togethers for a while.

New Living Arrangements (2001)

During the summer, at the beginning of August, when EJ and I spoke on the phone to check on each other, I told him how much I hated the student dorms and wished there was access to a kitchen, like in the student apartments.

Eventually, we came up with a plan for me to pocket all of my Pell Grant money by staying in his suite with him and whatever roommate he was assigned. In exchange, all I would have to do is be readily available whenever he needed a ride to the grocery store or back home to visit family, since he didn't have a vehicle. Consequently, I would have to leave the bulk of the items I accumulated during my freshman year at my uncle's house. The plan was for me to use a blow-up mattress we had and bring only clothes and any other necessities I needed. Luckily, I was a pro at improvising, and it wasn't a problem for me at all.

Once the first semester started, everything was smooth; EJ and I collaborated to ensure that neither of us was uncomfortable with the living arrangements. During the day, I would go to class and hang out around campus while EJ was either in class or at football practice. The only issue that would arise from time to time was when he planned to have female acquaintances come to the room.

Those evenings, I would tell him that I had no problem staying the night somewhere else, since I had friends around campus I could chill with. For most of those nights, this was the case, but there were a few occasions when I would end up sleeping in my car until I'd receive a "coast is clear" phone call from EJ, letting me know his company for the evening had left. At that point, I had already decided that next year I would apply for housing and obtain an official student apartment to live in.

The experiment with the Pell Grant Money wasn't worth the inconveniences it caused. As the first semester of my sophomore year progressed, I found myself focusing more on my studies and putting additional effort into academics compared to my freshman year. Yet, I'd still go to many of the on-campus parties and events. Other than that, I practically lived in the FAU library and the computer lab. During my downtime, when I wasn't studying or partying, I would dedicate time to writing raps, working out in the weight room, and playing pickup basketball during open gym hours. Don't get me wrong, I continued to stay in contact with a couple of female acquaintances off and on, but I didn't have time for anything serious until I met Nancy.

Unexpected Companion (2001)

I met Nancy in one of the Criminal Justice courses we were in together. We spoke occasionally, and after a few weeks of flirting, we exchanged phone numbers. We spoke on the phone often, and I'd even go visit her down in Fort Lauderdale (The Inveraray) since she didn't live on campus.

She was different from the others I'd come in contact with since I got to FAU because she was a seven-day Adventist. When I would go see her at the apartment that she lived in with her father, we'd always hang out and talk exclusively in the parking lot. Honestly, she was more reserved than I was used to, and when she explained her beliefs to me, I was taken aback, but I didn't shy away at all. When she told me about the lines she was unwilling to cross while seeing each other, she surely earned the utmost respect from me. Wholesome and a bit on the sassy side were two characteristics that intrigued me about her. She was good-looking and soft-spoken, but at that time, I felt that pretty girls came a dime a dozen at FAU. The fact that she was seemingly reserved was what I liked the most about her.

When I introduced Nancy to my friends and associates, they felt she wasn't the right one for me because we were polar opposites. To them, she was somewhat shy and quiet. I was labelled as the mischievous people person who was always on the scene around campus.

Apparently, it was all an act. The real Nancy would be revealed when superstar rapper Ludacris and his entourage came to the school to perform during the annual Freaker's Ball. The entire campus talked about the event the whole week before. Nancy and her best friend (who didn't attend our school) were all excited about the concert to the point that they were going out of their way to find "The right" outfits for the occasion.

During the night of the on-campus concert, Nancy told me she and her friend were invited to the after-party at the hotel where Ludacris and his entourage were staying.

I looked at her like she was crazy and said, "I can't believe you, of all people, are even considering going."

She responded by saying, "We just wanna go chill and hang out; nothing's going to happen!"

After a few seconds of deliberating, I told her, "Go have fun," in a quick, sarcastic tone.

It was at that moment that I would decide to ghost her and never deal with her again. Her attempts to contact me were met with either unanswered calls or one-to two-word responses whenever I decided to answer. She eventually got the point, and we wouldn't interact shortly afterward. I'd occasionally see her around campus, but I'd pretend as if she didn't exist. I knew I could've handled the situation better, but I could never grow accustomed to being disrespected by the ladies, given the things I'd experienced in the past.

Loss of a Loved One (2001)

In early November, tragedy struck again, this time closer to home than the previous situation. My beloved Aunt Sable was mysteriously murdered, and this incident completely flipped my family upside down. She was found in the duplex she was living in, totally naked and strangled to death. While the women in our family were grieving and vehemently seeking answers from law enforcement, the men in the family wanted instant revenge. Although the detectives were looking into possible suspects, my dad and my uncle were doing a little investigating on their own.

From what I was told, they were aggressively questioning a few of my aunt's old acquaintances. Come to find out, the detectives stated that through forensic evidence, they were able to discover two different strains of semen in her body. After the police questioned the two men, one of them left the state, and the other moved down to Monroe County. The case was never resolved due to a lack of substantial evidence, since there was more than one strain of DNA and no way to link the two suspects together.

The entire family was disappointed and distraught. All I could think about was the memories I had of her calling me "Mook," which was short for "Smookie," a nickname my dad used to call me when I was much younger. Many people from as far as Liberty City to the Bahas in Carol City loved my aunt. When she died, it left a huge hole in my heart that has never been filled. Hopefully, I'll be able to see her in Heaven when all is said and done.

A month later, after Auntie Sable's funeral in December, Granny had to have emergency surgery to have a few gallstones removed. They were causing her to experience serious discomfort in her stomach area. After she successfully went through surgery, I would call and visit her as much as possible to ensure that she was on the path to recovery. I couldn't imagine something happening to someone else, especially not a pivotal person in my family like Granny. The entire family made sure that she was well taken care of while she was in and out of the hospital. I'd speak with her every couple of days to let her know I was thinking of her. She reassured me that she was okay by stating, "Granny will be okay; God is good, just continue doing well in school." That was all I needed to hear.

I was determined to keep grinding in school to make something of myself in order to make Granny and my Aunt Sable proud. During that time, I remembered praying more consistently than ever because I was thankful that she was doing so well.

Creative Outlet (2002)

Since there was so much going on during this time, I had to divert some of my free time to something constructive. I found myself starting to slip back into some of my old ways from my freshman year, so I decided to put in more time into creating songs in my rap notebook. I wrote a few songs that dealt with the loss of my former high school teammate, Ray, and my Auntie Sable. I even wrote lyrics that randomly came to mind while I was sitting in EJ's room watching television or completing assignments for class. The more time I dedicated to writing, the better I got at it. Before I knew it, I remembered EJ coming to the room and randomly pointing at objects to see if I could include them in a freestyle.

One day, one of EJ's cousins, Kells, drove up to Boca Raton from Miami to visit, and he gave EJ a CD with some tracks he produced. Once he left, EJ and I listened to each of the tracks until one of them caught my attention. It was a fast-paced, up-tempo beat that reminded me of something that I'd heard before. Inspired, I immediately took out a pen and my notebook and started writing. I wrote the hook in 5 minutes, the first verse in 15 minutes, and the second verse in 10 minutes. EJ was shocked that I was able to come up with it in such a short period of time. He also wrote a verse to the song, but he didn't like how it sounded. That didn't stop him from calling his cousin and telling him that he had to hear what I wrote to one of his beats. Kells told us that we should come down south so he could hear it in person. Between EJ's demanding football schedule and my class schedule, we decided that we would take the drive to his studio at the beginning of Spring Break in March.

It was a Friday night when we arrived at an upscale condo in Aventura. We met Kells downstairs, and we took the elevator up to the studio. Once we got there, we noticed a short Hispanic male as well. He introduced himself as Reggie. Kells told EJ and me that we were officially at Mastermind Inc Studio, and they were ready to see what I had in store for them. I was extremely nervous internally, but externally, I gave off the appearance of a cocky and seasoned rap veteran.

When I got in the recording booth, they swiftly pressed play on the beat, and as soon as I got behind the microphone, I felt something come over me that was borderline spiritual, but in a negative way. From there, I could tell that I was about to embark on an out-of-body experience in the booth. As the pages turned in my notebook, Kells asked me for the title of the song, and I said, "B.O.B."

I could feel the pounding of the beat in my chest as the bass radiated through my headset. While I was rapping the first verse, I could feel the goosebumps popping up on my arms. I couldn't believe I was actually in a studio recording a rap song. When I finished the first verse and came out of the booth to hear the feedback, Kells, Chad, and EJ were all hyped and blown away because the way I completed the first verse was impressive. That night, I learned how to add ad-libs to a track and how to do double takes for the vocals. We were also able to record the entire song that evening, which only took a few hours. EJ impressively added some much-needed variety to the track by doing the hook, which was fast-paced and energetic.

Kells was so excited about the track that he wanted me to add verses to a reference track he produced for an unnamed female R&B group. The title of the track was "Jumpin'," and once I heard the beat he played for me, it only took me an hour to write the verses, and we recorded the entire song in two additional hours. The catchy hook was already done, and it featured the female vocalists singing, "The party's going on, and it's jumpin, jumpin, the party's going on, and it's jumpin!" The song sounded like something they would play on Power 96 in the evenings. Kells downloaded the tracks onto a couple of CDs and handed them to EJ and me so that we could have our own copies. When we left the studio, the sun was rising, and we felt that everything had gone extremely well. We were beyond excited.

A week or so afterward, we were invited back to the studio by Kells, who had devastating news. He told us that he sold the beat to the B.O.B song, and I would have to re-record the track with a new beat he created. We were so disappointed because we felt the song would've easily been a hit.

When he played the new beat for us, the first notion that came to mind was "This sh** is terrible, ain't no way this is going to work."

Kells tried to lighten the mood by telling us that Lenny Kravitz had heard the original song and potentially wanted to meet. In the back of my mind, I figured he was lying and just trying to distract us from the news he had just unloaded on us. After finishing up the few tracks we recorded, we left the studio totally dejected and utterly pissed off.

More Devastating News (2002)

On April 2nd, the day of my birthday, I received a call from my dad stating that Granny would need emergency surgery tomorrow because her doctor found cancer on a gallstone in her gallbladder.

After receiving the disturbing news, I went into a dark place, mentally. I couldn't help but start to question God. It seemed as if all my previous prayers fell on deaf ears. I still tried to celebrate my birthday and take my mind off what was going on with my grandmother, but nothing worked. During that time, I prayed more than I ever prayed in my life.

The next morning, I drove down to Jackson Hospital to await the results of Granny's surgery with the rest of the family. While we were in the lobby, the doctors came out to inform us that they had to remove her pancreas, part of her stomach, and part of her intestines. They also stated that she would have to go through eighteen months of chemotherapy. The most devastating news was the prognosis they provided, which was that she'd have at least one year to live, five at the most. It was a surreal moment that took a while for all of us to take in. Auntie Erica immediately stated she rebuked that prognosis in the name of Jesus!

We decided, as a family, that our prayers were going to be sufficient to help Granny beat those insurmountable odds. Thankfully, Granny's surgery was a success, and after a few days of recovering, she was allowed to go home. The doctor placed numerous restrictions on her that concerned me, as I realized Granny was known for her headstrong ways when it came to following anyone's advice or recommendations. The entire family would do their part to ensure that she was doing what she had to do on her end to recuperate, slowly but surely.

***

A few weeks after Granny's surgery, on the night of April 19th, I received a call from my cousin stating that one of our childhood homeboys, Stephen, was shot and killed! Stephen was the cousin of one of Lapolean's childhood friends from "Behind tha P," the same neighborhood in Opa Locka where Granny's house was located. Stephen was from another notorious neighbor, not too far from the Lake Lucerne community. Apparently, Stephen had his infant daughter in the car with him when he was shot to death, but she was unharmed during the fatal incident. I was beyond pissed off. To cope with the loss, I wrote a song called "My Profile," and I added a few choice lines about Stephen's untimely demise.

A week or so later, I would attend Stephen's funeral against the wishes of some of my family members, due to the unknown circumstances of his death. There were rumors that many of the people in Stephen's family were going to be out for revenge, and around those times, it wasn't uncommon for that to take place before, during, or after funerals in Miami. I made sure that I got to the church where the services were to be held extremely early so I could scope out the scene to ensure the coast was clear. I couldn't walk down the aisle to view Stephen's body in the casket because I wanted to remember him as the lively, extremely fashionable, and charismatic person he was, not in the state he was currently in.

The Return (June 2002)

After the end of my sophomore year in college, the week of Grace's high school graduation in Temple, Texas, we flew into town ready to pack her and my mom up and bring them back to South Florida for good.

When my father and I arrived at their apartment, the majority of their belongings were already packed in boxes, ready to go. My mom and sister had already rented the U-Haul truck that we would use to transport everything back to South Florida. After spending the first of June celebrating the excellent achievement my sister had accomplished of graduating from high school, the next day, my dad and I got into the U-Haul truck while my mom and sister got into their car and trailed behind us.

The drive from Texas to Florida took a full 24 hours to complete. It was the longest road trip that I've ever remembered taking in my life. Throughout the trip, we stopped a few times to eat, get gas, use the restroom, and take a nap at a public rest stop or two. When we finally made it to Miami, my legs felt so numb and weak; all I wanted to do was go inside the apartment, lie down, and stretch my legs until I fell asleep. That surely was a desire deferred due to my overly energetic father wanting to get all the items unloaded and put inside the apartment before the evening ended. He was adamant about returning the U-Haul truck by the next morning, since he only paid to rent it for a few days.

To be perfectly honest, my dad could be quite the penny-pincher. He would do anything to save a buck or avoid paying top dollar for anything. After spending hours unloading the truck, I abruptly grabbed my car keys from the countertop and headed toward the door. Everyone stopped what they were doing and asked me where I was heading off to. I responded by telling them I was headed to Uncle Stetson's house. The first thing they asked me was why, and I responded by stating, "I had some things to do." I lied. In actuality, I just needed a break from them after chilling with each other for so many days, nonstop. Things would've been better if we all had been able to gradually spend time together beforehand.

My dad's cheap, demanding ways were a pain; my mom started to annoy me with a million and one random questions, and my sister started to get on my nerves with her whining and complaining about everything. I knew that the one place I could go for peace and solace was my uncle's house. As I got ready to leave, I knew for a fact that my dad was pissed off with me for leaving, but he didn't say a word, for some reason. Though it wasn't like him, I appreciated the fact that he avoided the confrontational route he was typically so eager to take.

RIP Great-Grandma (2002)

On the 24th of June, I received a phone call that completely caught me off guard while driving up to Palm Beach to visit one of my college friends. One of my aunts called and stated that the family was at Aventura Hospital because Grandma Carol was having trouble breathing.

I inadvertently hit the brake pedal in my car and desperately looked for the closest exit on I-95. My plan was to get off heading northbound to get back on and head southbound. Once I completed that step, I noticed that I had one percent left on the battery of my phone and no phone charger in sight. I didn't want to grab my phone and start calling for updates because I knew that would drain the battery more. When I got halfway to the hospital, my phone died. Thankfully, I remembered my aunt telling me to come to the ER once I arrived. The biggest problem was that there was a series of accidents on I-95 that day. At some points during the drive, the traffic slowed to a crawl. I grew so impatient that I drove in the emergency lane off and on until I was able to get to the Aventura area.

All in all, it took me about an hour or so to get to the hospital. After that, when I didn't know if my family could take any more grief, my great-grandmother died from natural causes. Now, this incident hurt a lot because the way that I found out was horrible. The immediate family was supposed to meet up at the hospital in order to see how Grandma Carol was feeling. I guess everyone who was already there had left. After I eventually got there, I went to the front desk and asked the receptionist if I could see my great-grandmother, and she told me "Yes," like everything was fine, so I

167

went through the double doors and sat beside my great-grandmother in her room.

After I started talking to her, I noticed that she wasn't breathing at all; that's when I started to freak out. I started yelling, "What's wrong with my great-grandmother?" and I continued to repeat this so loudly that a nurse from next door came over and said, "Oh, they didn't tell you she died a little while ago." I was beyond devastated. Furthermore, I assumed that if a person died, then all potential visitors would be given a heads-up before entering their room, regardless of the past issues that my great-grandmother and I had while at Uncle Stetson's house. I still loved her. Every now and again, I find myself replaying the moment I found her lifeless body lying in a hospital bed, with the plastic tubing in her mouth. At that point, all I could ask myself was, "What's next?"

Wild Goose Chase (2002)

Toward the end of summer in July, I received a phone call that would raise my spirits a bit. It was EJ on the line, and he sounded overly excited. He cut to the chase and told me that he played the original B.O.B. song for our old high school classmate Alex. He said he liked it so much that he would set up a meeting between us and his relative, who was starting to become big in the music industry. It just so happened that his so-called relative was a popular Miami rapper named "Redd Eyezz."

The name rang a bell because he was also a prominent member of the Haitian organization known as the "Zoe Pound." I didn't respond too quickly because I was highly skeptical about the situation. On one hand, I was intrigued by the opportunity to meet and rub elbows with an artist generating a lot of buzz in the South Florida area. On the other hand, the reputation of "Zoe Pound" was nothing to play with either. Rumors about their organization made them infamous all over Florida. Due to all the deaths that I'd experienced over the past few years, I guess I was at my wit's end. I figured, "To hell with it! I might as well take some risks if I want to have a shot in the music industry." After a few seconds to deliberate, I told EJ I was cool with a meetup, but it would have to be during the daytime, not at night.

After hanging up, EJ called me back an hour later, saying that we were set to go pick up Alex tomorrow and drive down to the Overtown area in Miami to meet up with his people. After picking up EJ and Alex the next day, we headed down to meet Redd Eyezz. We pulled up to a neighborhood that seemed eerily quiet. Alex hopped out of the car and went to the front door of a house

169

that seemed as if no one was home. After a minute or two, he returned to the vehicle and stated that no one answered. So, EJ and I, out of sheer curiosity, asked him, "When was the last time you spoke to your cousin?" He sheepishly replied, "It's been a few years."

To avoid exploding with rage, I told Alex, "Come on, bro, let's go! I was visibly upset, though I did everything within my power to contain my disappointment. Alex was apologetic, and he started to give us a made-up story, but I wasn't trying to hear what he had to say. My primary focus was dropping him off as quickly as possible before I said or did something harmful to him. To be honest, I really wanted to slap the taste out of his mouth, but I showed restraint that day.

Junior Year at FAU (Aug 2002)

When I started the school year off, I legally moved into the student apartments, unlike my sophomore year. My roommate was a young man named Ryan. He and I started pretty well by establishing some clear-cut boundaries. He enjoyed chilling and smoking weed, so I advised him to smoke elsewhere because I didn't want the resident assistant or the campus police to raid our room and get us kicked out or worse. One day, while doing laundry in the shared laundry area, I noticed that one of the guys who used to live on the first floor in the dorm's freshman year had just moved to the apartments as well. Michael was an up-and-coming DJ known for making beats in his room. One evening, I went to his room to say, "What's up?" When I arrived there, I could hear that he was working on some mixes on his turntables.

After we dapped each other up, I asked him what he was working on. He told me he was working on a mix for an upcoming event. Then a beat from a popular song called "Grinding" by the rap group, "The Clipse," came on, and I couldn't resist the urge to freestyle. I asked him if he minded, and he told me to "Go for it," so I did. As the beat was about to end, I continued to freestyle until I was rapping a cappella, so he started playing other instrumentals while I kept going. Before I knew it, I was seven to eight minutes in, nonstop.

When I finally did, he yelled out, "Yooo, that was tight, bro! Oh My God!" He then asked me if I had ever made music before. I told him that I had recorded a song or two before, but it didn't take off as I had anticipated. He told me he had a few beats he was working on and suggested I see if I could create lyrics for them.

The two beats he played for me were hard-hitting and eerie. I told him I'd be right back as I sprinted out of his room towards my room in the building not too far away. I knew that that was probably a second chance at creating music again. I didn't want the opportunity to escape me again. My plan was to go to my room to grab my rap notebook and head back to Michael's room. When I returned, I immediately asked him for something to write with and started jotting down more lyrics to a song I was working on. I channeled all the turmoil and all the grief that I'd experienced throughout the past few years to create the type of songs that were really too explicit for mainstream radio. After that evening, at least a few days each week, I would go to Michael's room to work on music.

Double Vision (Sept 2002)

During the first week of September, when my college friends and I were all casually hanging out, a random beat came on a boom box one of my homeboys was using, and I started playfully freestyling about random items within our vicinity. Suddenly, Dee chimes in and starts freestyling as well. I was thoroughly impressed by the tone and the rhyme scheme he was able to put together on the spot. I asked him if he ever really rapped before; he stated that he writes from time to time. It was like a light bulb went off in my head, and I immediately told him that I knew someone who made beats, and on top of that, he was from Orlando, too. He was as intrigued as I was, so I took him to Michael's room, and luckily, he had just gotten back from grabbing something to eat.

After introducing the two of them, he played two of the beats to which I had already written two verses each.

Dee smiled and said, "Oh, I got something for those."

He also said, "I'll be right back" and ran to his room to get his rap notebook, which was the same reaction I had when I first heard Michael's beats, too. Some may refer to it as irony, but I like to call it fate. When Dee got back, he unleashed one of the most powerful flows and cadences I've ever heard in my life. If I were viewed as a good rapper, then Dee had to be superb.

From the first track, it was clear that Dee's skill set was far superior to mine in terms of natural talent and delivery. However, the funny thing was that our styles flowed so well together that Michael recommended Dee and me form a rap group. Ironically, Dee and I glared at each other and said, "Let's do it!" Luckily for me, Dee had time on his hands, considering that he wasn't playing basketball anymore due to issues with grades. So, Dee and I would often meet in my room to create and run clever lyrics by each other. We had one slight issue, though. We had to come up with the name of our group. In comes EJ; He came by my room one evening while we were in the creative stages of trying to determine a catchy name. He looked at both of us and said, "Y'all boys kinda look alike." I chimed in by stating that many people often mistake the two of us for each other around campus. Dee responded by agreeing that a few people thought he was me around campus. EJ said, "It's like seeing double." How about "Double Vision?" Dee and I exchanged smirks and yelled with excitement.

As far as we were concerned, now that we had a name, we could fully submerge ourselves into the grind of getting into the music industry. We would go on to write 15 to 16 songs to Michael's beats. I usually started most of the songs off with the first verse or two, but I had a superb knack for creating hooks. The problem we had was that we didn't have a professional studio to record our songs in. Michael told us to be patient; he would find a studio for us to go to.

In the meantime, we would continue to go to our classes, attend parties, and get into all sorts of mischief. While everyone I hung out with, other than EJ, smoked weed and drank liquor, I never smoked due to the trauma I went through from witnessing my father spiral out of control with his addiction. As far as drinking goes, my friends often strongly discouraged it by hiding the beverages from me. I was already rather lively, unpredictable, and slightly off-kilter back then, so alcohol would've caused me to potentially hurt myself or others by doing something stupid. I was a lightweight in the drinking department, so it didn't take anything strong to turn me up.

One weekend, there was a situation when Dee and I were hanging out with our crew of friends at the apartments. Many of our crew were hanging out, drinking, smoking, listening to music, cracking jokes, and so on. I thought it would be a great idea to sneak into the kitchen area and snag a few Smirnoff wine coolers. The funny thing about that situation was that everyone was given a heads-up that I was the only one to whom the drinks were off-limits. I felt they were overacting as usual.

After a few unsuccessful attempts, I finally got my hands on a few of them; five to be exact. The people who were supposed to be watching the drinks let their guard down, and I undoubtedly capitalized on the opportunity. A few seconds after downing the fifth wine cooler, I started feeling dizzy and disoriented. I quickly understood why they tried to keep me away from the beverages. I started tripping, to say the least. The next thing I remembered was waking up in the middle of the night, under my bed, with my shirt off. When my eyes opened, the first thing I could see was the bars under my bed; I thought I was in a jail cell for doing something strange after I started spazzing out on the multitude of wine coolers I had consumed. When I ran into my friends after that night, they told me that I had tried to rip a fire extinguisher off a wall, and I threatened to spray it until they intervened and persuaded me to go to my room.

Finally, in The Studio (Oct 2002)

After patiently waiting, Michael finally found a studio where we could record our tracks. It was located in a building just right outside of John I. Leonard High School in Greenacres. When we first arrived at the two-story office building, we walked up the steps to the corner suite without any outlandish expectations in our minds. Once we were escorted inside, we were pleasantly surprised by the decor and its professional look. Even though it wasn't my first time in a studio, this experience was a bit different. It was more legit than what I was accustomed to. From the lighting and the overall layout, it was downright immaculate.

Our first time in the studio was marred by a few technical issues with the instrumentals Michael brought with him. Therefore, he had to do some things to the tracks on his end, and we would eventually return to the studio the following week. We planned to record two of our top tracks to serve as a demo to attempt to go after a major record deal. Once we started recording one of our best tracks, it was like magic. During the second trip to the studio, we recorded one of our earlier songs called "Choppa Kingz." It took us a total of 4 hours to record the track to our liking, which cost us $160 ($40 an hour). At the follow-up studio session, the next week, we recorded our second track, "My Profile," while we were waiting for our first track to be properly mixed. Considering that this was our second session, the engineer told us that he would have both of the tracks burned onto a CD so we could play them whenever we wanted. The catch was that we would have to come back to pick up the disc the next day.

Once we got back, the next afternoon, we noticed that a couple of fellow FAU Owls (artists Dent and Logic) that we knew were in the studio finishing up their session. While we were waiting for our CDs, we jumped in the booth to record a freestyle session with them on a beat they were considering for their mixtape. After we finally received our music from the engineer, we returned to my car and blasted the songs repeatedly as we headed back to Boca. When we played the tracks for everyone who lived in the student apartments, the feedback was generally positive. After a while, word spread throughout campus that we had recently recorded songs, and Michael even set things up so we could perform at one of the upcoming on-campus parties.

***

Our First Live Performance

On the day of our upcoming performance, Dee and I spent a few hours going over all the specifics of what we would do during the event, from what we were going to wear to how we would perform and what song we'd use. Of course, I was more nervous than I'd ever been, considering this was going to be our first time displaying our talent in front of anyone. I believe Dee was more excited than nervous, since he was used to playing basketball in front of big crowds. We decided to play off the "Double Vision" name by wearing outfits that are somewhat similar but with slight differences. We would both wear long white T-shirts, black jeans, and shoes to match. Since my alter ego was to be the supposed "ladies' man" of the group, I would spice my attire up with accessories such as a headband, a gold necklace with a dollar sign pendant, and diamond earrings. Dee, on the other hand, was his alter-ego, a no-sense militant type. He wouldn't add any

177

accessories to his attire, even though he played with the idea of wearing a headband as well.

When we got to the venue, we noticed that it was jam-packed, wall to wall with people everywhere. The up-tempo music was pounding, and most of the attendees were vibrantly dancing and having a great time. DJ Skoobz and Michael were splitting time on the turntables, doing their thing as we approached. Michael saw us, smiled, dapped us up, and continued to play his mix to keep the crowd rocking and enjoying themselves. Toward the latter part of the party, he told the attendees that there was a special performance that he had in store for them. After a few more songs had been played, we were given "the signal," which indicated that it was time to come and get the two microphones that were near the speakers.

Once we grabbed them and the instrumental for our "My Profile" song began to play, I immediately ripped into the track with the intensity of a Mack truck speeding down a highway. After I finished the first two verses of the song, and it was Dee's turn to rap his verse, the track abruptly skipped repeatedly and totally derailed the rest of our performance. In short, we didn't get a chance to finish our song that night. We were beyond disappointed, and Michael was extremely apologetic afterward, though we didn't necessarily want to hear it. We felt that was a blown opportunity, and we for sure did not like the fact that we felt like we failed.

***

As we were getting ready to leave the Live Oak Pavilion, there was a young lady named Monica who gave me her phone number before I hit the exit. Even though I didn't know her directly, I remembered seeing her in passing at different events on campus. I also heard stories about her previously dealing with a few members of the football team, including one of my associates. That evening, after calling the number she gave me, we chatted for a bit, and less than an hour later, I convinced her to come to my room "to chill." Her only reservation was that she didn't want to be seen coming to my room so late at night. Since I was on the first floor and my bed was located in the back corner of the room, I advised her that she could always come around the back and climb through my window. I wasn't really serious about the suggestion, but when she said, "Okay, I can do that," I just went with it. I couldn't help but think, "Damn, I can't believe she actually agreed to it. Oh well!"

When she arrived at my window, I immediately let her in, and we spent a few hours or so together. Afterward, she left the same way she came in. From there, we would begin to talk on the phone frequently. Monica wasn't a student at FAU; she attended Palm Beach State Community College, which was located behind my school. I eventually asked her about the "situation ships" she was rumored to have had with some of the people I knew, and she confirmed one of the two. She told me that she never took things "to that level" with anyone I was friends with. Unsurprisingly, she also told me that she was in the process of breaking up with her boyfriend, who was away playing football at a college in California. Something told me that maybe she had too much going on at the time, but I disregarded all of those issues. Since she looked like she could've been a centerfold for Jet Beauty Magazine, I decided to give things a chance. I guess you could call it, "Acting like a person who never had nothing!" Or maybe I was just mesmerized by her physique.

***

Meeting an Icon

After the botched performance, we took a few days to process what transpired. One of our associates, named Danny, who was a member of the football team, told us that one of his "peoples" was Miami Rap Legend, JT Money. He also told us that we should come down to his mother's crib in Miami so that we could meet him in person. So, one afternoon during Thanksgiving break, Dee and I drove down to the house to meet the Miami Legend. But once we arrived, Danny told us something had come up, and he was unable to meet up. Danny told us that he would still give him a copy of our demo CD to check out when he saw him again. Disappointment, yet again.

When we left, we didn't say much about the situation to each other. Dee and I spent so much time together leading up to that moment that, after a while, we knew when it was time to converse and when to be silent. As we rode back to Boca, we let the music playing in my car do all the talking for us, since none of us had anything to say. When we finally made it back to campus, the last track of Soulja Slim's "The Streets Made Me" album was just about finished playing, and we dapped each other up and went to our separate rooms. Dee went to smoke, and I went to hop on the phone with Monica.

The Main Thing (2002)

Since my popularity was pretty high, one of my female friends recommended that I run for Homecoming King. At first, I scoffed at the idea, but then some of my homeboys told me I might as well because everyone either knew me or knew of me. So, after a bit of leg pulling and an impromptu speech from a friend about the need for diversity in the homecoming court, I decided to throw my hat in the ring.

Coincidentally, one of the young ladies who was also running was originally from Miami. We decided to campaign together. We were cool through a mutual friend, so running together wasn't awkward, even though I knew Monica would feel some way about it. During the week of homecoming, I attended all the festivities, such as the homecoming dance and the homecoming football game, where they introduced the homecoming court. We didn't win homecoming king and queen, but we did become homecoming prince and princess.

After the game, I noticed that Monica and her friend Mikayla were at every event, eyeballing me like a hawk. I could feel the jealousy oozing from their eyelids. There was hell to pay when I made it back to my apartment, to say the least. After Monica came in and quickly went on a rant about me looking like I was "so happy." She made comments that indicated that she didn't enjoy seeing another female close to me, as if I were her property. I told her that she couldn't be too mad at me, regardless of the fact, since she had a whole boyfriend up in Cali. It was then that she told me she had called him and said their relationship was over. I didn't believe her at first, but after a while, she would do subtle things to prove that she was indeed telling the truth.

What was once intended to be a one- or two-night stand quickly turned into a relationship. I went from sneaking her into my apartment through a window late at night to meeting her parents. I would grow to realize she was what I needed to set aside some of my immature ways and focus on the future. Not only that, but I'd never really considered really settling down after Crystal broke up with me during freshman year. I knew I couldn't continue stacking the type of body count I'd been acquiring since then. Many of my friends advised me not to get into a serious relationship with her because of her reputation around town. Still, they knew I was hard-headed and would do whatever I wanted, regardless.

We kept each other motivated academically, and from time to time, I would have to make trips to her school to protect her from the occasional harassment of male students who'd get a little too pushy while attempting to talk to her. I wasn't aware of what I was getting myself into, dealing with a young lady of her caliber. At every major event we went to, dudes would stop and stare or get downright rude and disrespectful. I would find myself getting into arguments and confrontations because people couldn't believe she was with someone like me, for some reason.

Christmas Break (2002)

During my break from school, I was able to spend some time with my parents and my sister. Though I had my reservations about the two of them reuniting after all these years, I was happy to witness all the hard work and dedication my dad put towards ensuring that the logistics were sorted out. I ended up dividing my time between my dad's spot and my uncle's, depending on what I had going on at the time. I put some serious mileage on my new car, traveling all around Dade County, without a preplanned destination, usually just "riding and looking."

I enjoyed driving since it gave me an excuse to roll my windows down while blasting my music as loud as possible. Not only that, but I guess one could say, "I was showing off in my new whip." My usual riding partner was Kevin, one of my friends/teammates from high school. Occasionally, we'd stop by P's house in the northern part of the city and Yattis' family's apartment in the Lincoln Field Apartments. When we would stop by P's house, he always had something interesting going on. He was either working on a car's sound system or cracking jokes at someone who was visiting him.

At Yattis's spot, he was always watching WWF wrestling, watching a classic movie, or playing Madden. I used to marvel at the gold-plated championship wrestling belts he had strategically placed throughout his bedroom. He was another one of the homeboys who was hilarious to be around. He had a way of delivering vivid details during his storytelling sessions that reminded me of comedians like Bernie Mac or Robin Harris from back in the day. Yattis was also a resourceful individual. Thanks to his connections in the inner city, I got a sweet three-hundred-dollar deal on a speaker case containing four "Kicker" 12-inch subwoofers with a 2000-watt 4-channel amplifier from one of his homeboys. The only catch to the purchase was that I had to find someone to hook it all up.

On the other side of town, the only person I knew who had the expertise and experience that I'd actually trust to do the job was P. He was a pure wizard with sound systems. As a matter of fact, when we were in high school, I remember seeing him pull up in an old-school car playing music that radiated throughout the student parking lot. Once he popped the trunk, we all noticed that he was crafty enough to take a set of house-stereo speakers and successfully connect them to his car's audio system. That was the distinct memory that came to mind immediately before I decided to take my car and newly acquired speaker system to P for installation. After connecting the system, he informed me that I needed a separate amplifier for the "mids and highs" (speakers) located in the interior.

After going to Brands Mart to acquire the amplifier my friend suggested I get, I had their installation personnel attach it to the speaker box in my trunk. Afterward, they carefully ran the heavy-duty electrical wiring from the amplifier to my car stereo. After they were done, I was officially ready to ride out and go cruising all over town. Everywhere I went, people could hear me coming well before they could see me. The amount of base that came from the trunk was devastatingly loud and obnoxious, just the way many of us from South Florida liked it.

Another Accident (2002)

On New Year's night, before the end of the Christmas break, Kevin and I went to South Beach to ride around and check out the scenery on the strip. We hung out until late at night, and on our way back to my uncle's house, we decided against taking I-95 all the way there. We decided to take 27th Avenue the majority of the way there.

We were so tired that we both fell asleep at many of the red lights we stopped at. Thankfully, around that time, not too many people were on the road. When we finally made it halfway to County Line Road, I turned up the music substantially, rolled all the windows down, and attempted to wake myself up to make it back to the house in one piece. After a few seconds, I fell asleep again while driving. This time, I was awakened by fiery sparks flying in the air on the passenger side of the car as I slid against a guardrail. We were right beside the canal along University and Miramar Parkway. Kevin and I frantically searched and panicked after exchanging a few choice words. I quickly pulled over to the nearby IHOP parking lot to assess the damage and easily saw the indentation left by the guardrail on the side of my car. I was beyond pissed off at myself.

When we finally arrived at my uncle's house, I went to the garage, grabbed a can of white spray paint, and covered the damaged portion of my car so it wouldn't look too noticeable. Everyone was already sleeping by the time we made it back, so we didn't say anything to my uncle about the accident. I knew I would have to tell him eventually, but at least I could sleep on it and then figure out how I would break the news.

The next morning, when I woke up and went into the living room, I noticed that Kevin was no longer lying on the couch, and my uncle wasn't in his room either. I could hear two distinct voices coming from the driveway outside. Once I realized that it was indeed Kevin and my uncle out there, all I could think was, "Oh my God, he knows already." I told myself, "Well, might as well go outside and face the music."

As I opened the door and walked outside to find out what they were talking about, I heard hysterical laughter instead of disappointed anger. Apparently, Kevin and my uncle were both outside looking at the terrible job I'd done of trying to cover up what happened to the car with cheap spray paint. My uncle, with his eyes nearing bulging out of his head, was looking at me like I was insane. While Kevin was chuckling about the events from the night before, I just knew my uncle was going to give me one of his hour-long speeches, but he didn't. Apparently, Kevin had already filled him in on the accident that occurred, so there wasn't much more to say.

Unsurprisingly, I was asked about the spray paint, and the only thing I could come up with was to shrug my shoulders, laugh, and say that I was trying to make the damage "not so noticeable." He told me that I made it more noticeable since the original color of the car was a different shade of white than the spray paint I used. Last night, it seemed fine, but when I looked at it in the sunlight, I could clearly see that my uncle was right; it didn't match at all. I was so ashamed that I couldn't do anything but join the two of them in laughter. The main thing that I would have to wrap my mind around was returning to school with a huge gash on the side of my car. I knew that many of my friends and associates would ask me a bunch of questions that I would be too embarrassed to answer.

***

Returning to College

I was nervous pulling up to the student apartments, so I intentionally drove my car in a manner where onlookers couldn't see the dent on the passenger side. When word got out that I had a wreck, word spread like wildfire. I knew I shouldn't have told too many people what actually happened, though I had a habit of running my mouth too much whenever I began to passionately describe a situation that recently occurred (The same way I passionately recited the rap lyrics in Dee and I's songs).

***

Attempted Redemption

When I met up with Dee, and we went to Michael's room, he said he had some exciting news for us. He told us that he knew the owner of Club Radius (later known as Club Boca), and he was able to hook it up so Dee and I could perform our music. The week of the performance, we practiced how we'd do everything just like the last time we performed. When the day of showtime came, we were more than ready. We told Michael to make sure the music was on point. On our way to the club, we played the CD with our instrumentals to ensure there wouldn't be any hiccups when it was time to go on stage.

Once we arrived, we noticed that the parking lot was full. As we walked into the club, we saw many people we knew from FAU. We also noticed that a well-known DJ named Tech was in the DJ booth doing his thing. Apparently, the ICONZ, a popular up-and-coming rap group out of Miami, was supposed to perform their hit single, "Get Crunked Up," after we performed. Something happened, and we were told they had to perform before us because they had to leave. When they performed, the crowd was turned up and reciting their lyrics the entire time. The pure energy from the performance was infectious. We knew it would be a tough act to follow.

When it was time for Dee and me to show the crowd what we had in store for them, we grabbed the microphones and hit the stage as Michael introduced us from the DJ booth. When the instrumental came on to our "My Profile" song, we paced back and forth on the stage like we owned it. Dee started with the ad-libs as I started rapping the first verse. I could see all the people who knew us, supporting us smack-dab in front of the stage. After my first verse, Dee and I recited the hook, and the crowd got into it. As I got into verse two, I could tell the guys who were in the club were listening to every lyric intently to hear the message I was delivering, while the young ladies were vibing to the beat. When we got to the hook again, some of the spectators in the crowd started chanting along, which was one of the best feelings in the world. I felt so empowered.

Then it happened again. As Dee began rapping his verse, the beat switched up a bit, and then, without warning, the music unexpectedly cut out as soon as Dee said, "To the death of me," to start his first bar; that was it. It was the same thing that occurred at the party at FAU. We handed the microphones to Michael after we left the stage and beelined toward the exit.

When we got to my car, many of our friends met us in the parking lot to console us, but we weren't trying to hear anything they had to say. As we drove back to the apartments, we voiced our frustrations to one another. We hung out and chilled with a few of our friends for a bit at the student apartments until we called it a night and went our separate ways to our rooms to try to put the previous situation behind us. A little later, Monica called to check on me while she was driving home. As she sensed the disappointment in my voice, she decided to come over to console me.

The Devil's Lettuce (2003)

The following week, my roommate Ryan and I got into a heated back-and-forth about him smoking in our room when I wasn't there. He swore me up and down that he wasn't doing so, but I could smell it lingering throughout the bathroom area. So, in retaliation, I decided to wait until he left the room for class and thoroughly search our bathroom area for any paraphernalia that he might've been hiding in there. After searching for a few minutes, I found a small black pouch with a small baggie of marijuana inside. I knew I'd find something, but that didn't cause me to feel less irritated or upset.

The first idea that came to mind was revenge. I considered throwing the drugs away until I came up with the dastardly and potentially dangerous plan to take the marijuana out and lightly dip it in the liquid laundry detergent. After barely submerging the weed in the detergent, I grabbed a paper towel from the kitchen countertop. I patted it dry, so it wouldn't be noticeable upon going back into the baggie. I didn't really think about the potential severity of my actions, since I was extremely pissed off that he continued to disrespect me by smoking in our room. After putting his weed back where I found it, I left the room for the rest of the day. I knew he would return from class soon, and I didn't want to be there when he got back. My goal was to seem as unsuspicious as possible and go about my usual daily routine.

I went to Dee's room and told him what was going on, and he looked at me, laughed, and said, "Baybay, you tripping dog! You could kill that man! What are you thinking about, bro?" I responded, "Naw, he'll be alright. He shouldn't have tried me, I told him not to smoke in our room, he's lucky I didn't swing on him." Dee then stated, "You wildin', bro!" Then we started talking about music and other things happening around the campus.

A day later, all seemed well. Ryan didn't say a word about his detergent-soaked marijuana, even though I know he must've found it by then. It was seemingly a typical day, so I went about my business and ventured down the hall to holler at my friends Denise and Joan. Dee just so happened to be there to see if they had some juice.

When they said, "No,"

He asked if I had juice in my room, and I said, "Yes!"

I tossed him my room key, and he went down to get some. About 1 to 2 minutes later, he came back with a light jog toward us and said,

"Aye Baybay, you won't believe what your roommate did! I'm about to kill this man!"

I said, "Who, Ryan?"

Apparently, as retaliation for his detergent-soaked weed, Ryan peed in my fruit punch container, shook it up, and returned it to the refrigerator. Dee said that as he was pouring a glass of juice, he noticed the strange suds in the clear container that were unusual. Afterward, he said he put the rim of the container close to his nose and inhaled, discovering the distinct smell of urine. He also told me that Ryan was in the room, so he poured the cup of juice he was about to drink into the sink and left the jug on the countertop for me to check out for myself.

Upon returning to my room, ironically, Ryan had already conveniently left before I got there. When I took the lid off the jug

191

of juice, the aroma of urine was faint but noticeable. I immediately left the room to tell Dee, Denise, and Joan that he did indeed pee in my juice container!

I was beyond livid as I confirmed Dee's initial prognosis. I told them that I was going to kill him whenever he got back to the room. My friends gave me excellent advice at that time. They told me to do what he would more than likely do if the shoe were on the other foot. I knew exactly what they meant without going into further detail, so I placed two phone calls: one to the non-emergency police line and the other to the Resident Assistant. The police dispatcher stated that they were sending out an officer, and the R.A wasn't in his room at the moment.

As we waited outside for the police to arrive, Dee and I grew angrier by the minute. We kept thinking about the fact that any of us could've drunk the urine-infused juice if Dee had never discovered it. After the police arrived, we told them our individual accounts of what happened. They wrote our statements down and then went to the room to question my roommate. Apparently, he admitted to the terrible deed, though he didn't mention anything about the detergent/weed situation. I advised the officers that my issues with him stemmed from his constantly telling Ryan not to smoke in the room. They asked for his permission to search his side of the room, and they were able to find traces of marijuana residue and other paraphernalia in his dresser. The officers told me that Ryan told them that he heard that I kept a firearm stashed in my car. Not only that, but I supposedly kept it hidden within the speaker box in my trunk.

When the officer questioned me about it, I laughed and offered to take him to my car to check. He obliged, and when we made it to the student parking lot, I eagerly popped the trunk because I knew that I didn't have a firearm. If I did have one, I told the officer that I wouldn't have been stupid enough to keep a firearm in a hot speaker box with electrical equipment. I offered to get a screwdriver to unscrew one of my four speakers so he could have a look inside the box himself, but he declined, and we returned to the main corridor of the apartments.

The officer was able to get in contact with the R.A and, after further discussion, Ryan was ordered to get his belongings and move out of our room. After, I found out that he was kicked out of the student apartments for the rest of the year. The best thing that came from that situation was that I no longer had a roommate, giving me the entire room to myself for the rest of the semester.

The End (Feb 2003)

Dee and I had taken a couple of weeks' hiatus from making music due to the discouraging setbacks that had taken place recently. He started to hang out more and more with Edward, who was also deep into selling and smoking weed heavily.

As for me, my focus was more on keeping my grades up to graduate on time the following year. Besides, Michael was preoccupied with pledging to be in a fraternity. It was a secretive process that no one was supposed to know about, but somehow, I knew what was going on behind the scenes. Occasionally, Dee would swing by his room to listen to some of the latest beats he created, and Dee could see that Michael's focus was elsewhere because the quality wasn't what he was accustomed to hearing from him.

One night, Dee and Edward were stopped by the police while having a bunch of weed in Edward's car. Instead of allowing the officers to pin the weed on Edward and having his truck towed, Dee told them that the drugs were his and his alone. They allowed Edward to go, and they took Dee to the jail on Gun Club Road.

The next morning, I received a phone call from a number I didn't recognize, and I just so happened to answer it out of sheer curiosity. It was Dee calling me from a pay phone near a 7-Eleven, telling me that he was released on "OR" (Own-Recognizance). He asked me to come pick him up, and I immediately jumped in the Chevy to get him. Once I made it to his location, we stopped by a Burger King to grab him a bite to eat before heading to the student apartments. While on the way, he told me everything that led up to

194

his arrest, as well as what transpired while he was briefly incarcerated. From there, I could look in his eyes and tell that there was a change in him from that point forward.

A week or so later, we had a conversation where he informed me that he'd be returning home to Orlando and that he knew it was time for a spiritual change. I asked him what he was going to do with all his music, and he responded by saying, "I'm not going to do nothing with the music." I knew that was the best thing for him, so I dapped him up, told him I understood, and advised him that I would be there for him whenever he needed me.

From that point on, all things related to making music stopped, and I turned all my attention to academics and my relationship with Monica.

Senior Year (2003-2004)

The pressure was at that time since it was my senior year. I had to consider what the future might hold for me. I contemplated taking the LSAT to get into law school, but I knew the pressure would be on me to make money after graduating, as I didn't want to return to Miami to figure things out from there. There were a few huge tasks that I had to take care of before I could begin to worry about any of that.

The main task would be satisfying the Spanish 2 requirement for my major. The year before, I passed Spanish 1 by the seat of my pants. I knew the course would be more strenuous and nerve-racking than last year's course.

On the first day, as I walked in, I noticed that the professor was a middle-aged Hispanic lady with a strong accent. While she was reviewing the various aspects of the course, she stated that by week two, all students will be expected to speak Spanish at all times to communicate. At that moment, I realized it would be better to take the course at Palm Beach State because of the smaller teacher-to-student ratio. (I always heard Spanish 2 was an easier course at the community college level, according to some of my peers.) I was able to successfully pass the course with a lot of hard work and dedication. The course professor allowed my classmates and me to work on many of our assignments in groups, which proved to be extremely beneficial.

Another issue I had to deal with wasn't as difficult, just time-consuming. My academic advisor told me that any student who was a Criminal Justice major had to fulfill a requirement that consisted of taking part in a semester-long internship. After receiving the surprising news, I quickly contacted the Boca Raton Police Department to inquire about a potential internship, and the coordinator advised me on what I had to do. Step #1: I had to apply for an internship. Step #2: The department had to conduct a background check on me. Step #3, I'd have to take a lie detector test at the police department.

Thankfully, I was able to make it through the preliminary portion of the process successfully. I was scheduled to take the mandatory lie detector test in 24 hours. I was so nervous since I'd never taken one before. I only heard stories about them on television shows and movies. I could only imagine what type of questions they'd ask me, which was a little concerning due to my questionable upbringing and checkered past over the last few years.

Monica told me not to worry, just be truthful, and everything would take care of itself. That was one of the reasons why I'd end up falling in love with her. She supported me regardless of whether I was right or wrong, and that was something I wasn't used to. She also didn't judge me based on my past, and I tried not to do the same to her, even though it seemed extremely difficult.

On the day of the scheduled lie detector test, I practiced specific breathing exercises I found online and followed that up with a lot of prayer. When I arrived at the police department, I was dressed to kill. I wanted to leave a good first impression when I was seen at the station. I waited in the lobby for about fifteen to twenty minutes.

When the technician called me to the room for the test, I outwardly appeared cool, calm, and collected; internally, I was the exact opposite. As I sat down, electrodes and wraps were placed on my fingers and arms. The technician started off by asking me very simple questions, such as whether my name was Fernando or not. Then he went from basic to more elaborate, intrusive questions, such as "Have I been arrested or detained for any crimes within the past year or so," and "Are you an acquaintance of any known felons?" I was more fearful of not passing and risking not graduating on time than I was of possibly facing ridicule for the answers I gave. My main concern was the nervousness; none of my responses were flagged for deception.

All in all, I ended up passing the test, and I was granted entry into an internship with the Victim Advocate Department of the police department. The ladies who ran the unit were very nice as they walked me through their roles and day-to-day responsibilities. The internship wasn't what I expected, and it was rather boring, to be honest. They kept me in the office doing little miscellaneous tasks to occupy my time. It helped me make up my mind about possibly working in a police department. Some of the sidebar conversations that I heard let me know that many cops aren't as noble and honorable as the media makes them seem on television.

The strange part about everything was the fact that I wouldn't have thought in a million years someone would allow someone like me in a police station around confidential files, considering all that I've done and been through.

New Living Arrangements (2004)

Upon completion of my internship, Monica and I moved into an off-campus apartment in Boca Raton. It was a huge leap in our relationship that my grandma advised me against taking. She would often tell me that I shouldn't "Shack up" with a female who I'm not married to. In hindsight, she was correct.

During the first few months, while I was finishing up my senior year in college, everything was cool. However, things would go sour after a while once I discovered that Monica and I were operating at two different wavelengths. Her primary focus was on her looks and her managerial job in customer service, and I was constantly looking for ways to elevate. Something that caught me off guard about her was that, through a little snooping and investigating, I found out that she had an affinity for athletes from the area. When we spent a lot of time at her parents' home, there were many reminders all around hinting at the notion that she was known as a bit of a social butterfly, to say the least. Regardless of her past, I tried to put all the evidence and information I discovered on the back burner. My goal was to mold her into the type of woman I always wanted, even though my attempts were totally unsuccessful. The frustrating part was that I wanted her to fit a standard that I wasn't even able to fulfill myself.

After a while, we clashed, argued, and fought more than we ever did before. I quickly discovered that the older generation was right: "You won't really know a person's true colors until you live together." I figured I'd try to make things better by fully committing to her, but after the allure of a new beginning wore off, it was back to the same chaos and anarchy as before. One of the biggest issues was that I felt that everything she'd tell me was a lie. I would ask her questions about people or situations from her past to see what she'd tell me. 90% of the time, she'd lie or purposely leave out certain details. The worst part about it was that I already knew the answers to the questions I'd ask before asking them.

As for her family, which was a bright spot, they loved and considered me a good addition, but my severe frustrations with Monica's shortcomings were getting to me every day. I'd found myself cooking, cleaning, and essentially doing everything, while she went to work throughout the week. After a while, I would catch myself doing many domestic things around the house just to throw them in her face later. I unjustly judged her because she wasn't where I felt she should be at that time, as far as a potential wife was concerned. I was a complete jerk, but deep in my heart, I knew she didn't deserve the treatment I was giving her.

As I was nearing my graduation day, I also had a part-time job as a security guard at a local apartment complex in Boca Raton.

A Prized Possession (June 2004)

Unfortunately, my family and I received devastating news that Granny and Grandpa Theodore were losing their house in Opa Locka. Apparently, Granny had taken out a few mortgages on the house to support her gambling habit. Everyone knew that she loved to gamble, though no one knew just how bad it had gotten. The bank gave them a deadline to move their things out before they repossessed the property. My uncle, Aunt Teresa, and Aunt Erica all came together to help them secure a townhouse.

The day I went over to their new residence, I remembered trying to fight back tears. I couldn't believe the place where we all used to come together and spend time with one another no longer belonged to the family. So many memorable moments and milestones were celebrated there. The new spot wasn't too shabby, and Granny tried to downplay the entire situation by telling me that the old house had become too much to manage. She had a knack for stretching the truth a bit when it came to talking to her grandchildren. She would always give us the PG version of actual stories because she sincerely believed in the adage, "A child should stay in a child's place." I'm not saying that Granny was lying to us when she told my cousins and me anything. I'll chalk it up to "stretching the truth" a bit to protect our hearts and our minds. Based on her track record, I wasn't surprised that she didn't want me to know the actual story behind why she and Grandpa had to move.

As I got older, I discovered that there were many things that she attempted to hide from us, like the fact that 5 out of 6 of our aunts and uncles had different fathers. Something I didn't learn until I was in high school, but heard it wasn't so uncommon back in the day. After deep consideration, I assumed she might be ashamed or embarrassed, or perhaps she wanted better for us and didn't want to indirectly encourage certain behaviors, which would've made sense if that was the case.

Graduation (Aug 2004)

At the time of graduation, I was simultaneously happy and scared! The last four years were a whirlwind, but I didn't think I was ready for the real-world responsibilities that came with leaving college. My graduation day came and went quickly. A few of my family members were in attendance, and they got a chance to take many photos. We all went to Red Lobster to celebrate.

I knew my first order of business would be to find a career in the Criminal Justice field. Joan, one of my friends from college, advised me to contact the company that she was working for at the time. Pride Integrated Services had a contract with Palm Beach County to oversee all misdemeanor probation cases as well as the DUI Traffic School. I went through the application process, and when the day of my interview came, I completely crushed it. The interviewer loved the way I answered the questions so much that I was offered the job as a probation officer, on the spot.

Probation Officer (2004-2007)

When I first started as a probation officer, I was extremely overwhelmed due to the seriousness of the position. Managing each probationer's case files wasn't too difficult, but many of the interactions with them were something serious, to say the least. Many of the repeat offenders and "probation veterans" could immediately tell I was a rookie. I barely had any facial hair at the time, so I looked younger than I actually was.

For the first couple of weeks, I would get tried repeatedly. They would try all sorts of things, from attempting to talk their way out of potential random drug or alcohol testing to others trying to get me to accept fraudulent community service hours. After a while, word would get out that I wasn't tolerating any foolishness, and I'd shut them down quicker than a judge in a courtroom (no pun intended). Since I was the only male at our particular location, I felt the need to serve as the unofficial protector of the women in our office. Whenever a male probationer raised their voice with the other probation officers, I'd often walk by their office and ask whether or not everything was alright. Oftentimes, they'd tell me they're good, they can handle it. There were a few times when I would be taken up on my offer to assist them, especially when they were faced with someone overly aggressive. Thankfully, I never had to put my hands on anyone while working there, even though there were certainly many close calls.

Some other things would happen during my three years there that I wasn't prepared for; one of them was running into former college friends and acquaintances who came into the office for their monthly probation meetings. One particular situation that came to mind was when one of my homies, named Jorge, from my former college's football team, came in for his monthly visit. When I went to the lobby and called his name, he jumped out of his seat and said, "I know that ain't who I think it is! Baybay, what's up, bro?" I swiftly put my index finger over my mouth to indicate to him that he needs to keep his cool until I walk him back to my office. Once we got there, we caught up for a bit, and then I asked him about the misdemeanor possession charge for which he was on probation. He told me that the police caught him with "a little weed" and gave him six months of probation with an early termination option after a month, as long as all his court fees were paid and the drug course he needed to take was completed. Jorge couldn't believe I was a probation officer, considering the way I acted while in college.

Something else that took some time getting used to was going to the South County Courthouse a few times per week for people who either violated the terms of their probation or were being placed on probation after their sentencing. We all had set days when we would go to court. One thing I had to keep in mind constantly was that at any time, any one of us (probation officers) could get called to the courthouse for high-priority cases, so every day, other than Fridays, I would dress to impress with nice slacks and a button-up shirt and the trusty black leather coat my mom purchased for me. I also had a black leather bag that I'd use to carry any necessary case files or documentation in. I enjoyed dressing professionally and feeling important, even though I deeply despised having to occasionally speak in court amongst people I didn't know. Most of the days in court were extremely eventful, and I had the chance to rub elbows with lawyers, defense attorneys, state prosecutors, judges, judicial assistants, bailiffs, and even court reporters and translators. I appreciated the networking I was able to do while fulfilling an important role within the community.

Many strange and interesting things would take place in the courtroom, from Judge Hafele chastising disrespectful courtroom personnel, defendants, or spectators, to people having medical emergencies during non-jury trials. The courtroom really was a microcosm of society. Honesty, from inside "The System," it appeared to be all about the money rather than a true deterrent to committing a crime. Probation was basically a setup because the odds are usually unfavorably stacked against the probationer. In DUI cases alone, probationers would end up spending thousands of dollars between court fees, the monthly cost of supervision fees paid directly to the probation office, the cost of the DUI course, and the occasional drug/alcohol testing. Not to mention, their driver's license would be suspended for six to twelve months pending completion of particular requirements. Even after completing all their required tasks and receiving their driver's license back, they would still need to have an ignition interlock device installed on their car (which they would pay for weekly) for a predetermined period. The trick with the ignition interlock was that you had to breathe into a plastic tube periodically. If there were traces of alcohol on your breath, the car would immediately shut off wherever you were. That process was understandable but potentially very dangerous.

The worst aspect of the job, though, was the pay. One would think that with a position like ours, we would be well taken care of; that was the farthest thing from the truth. Between Monica's job and mine, we were the very definition of living paycheck to paycheck. Fortunately, I saved up a nice little nest egg from the past two years of receiving financial aid and Pell grant money while at FAU. The funds really came in handy when it came time to get a new vehicle.

Something New (2004)

The Chevy I worked hard to purchase was on its last legs, and it was time to upgrade from the car I loved in college, which had 20-inch chrome-spoke rims and four 12-inch speakers in the trunk. When I would go to court for work, I'd often park as far away from the actual courthouse as possible to avoid drawing too much attention to myself.

While on the ride home from work one day, I passed by an Ed Morse car lot that was located off Federal Highway. I unexpectedly saw a smooth-looking used 2003 champagne-colored Chevy Impala. When I pulled into the dealership, I cut to the chase and asked the salesman how much the car cost. He gave me a great deal on it that I couldn't refuse. Evidently, the car formerly belonged to a female senior citizen who no longer needed it. It had very low mileage, and both the interior and exterior were well-maintained. I was also able to purchase the car with little to no money down and a $250 per month payment. My next quest would be to find a buyer for my Chevy Caprice.

After speaking with my Godson's father, Billy, I decided to sell it to him, as is, for a couple of grand. It was tough letting it go, considering that it was my first car and my most expensive purchase to date. There were so many memories that I had in it that I felt like I was letting a member of my family go. The good thing was that it was at least going to someone I knew. The new car took some time getting used to. I had factory speakers, the original factory car stereo, and regular Chevy hubcaps. It was so plain and so basic that I knew if I didn't do anything else, I would have to upgrade the sound system. So that's what I did. I went straight to

Brands Mart and purchased a black Kenwood CD player and a speaker box with two BOSE 12-inch speakers, since I let Billy have the system. When I played my music in the new car, there was a big difference between what I'd grown to love over the years up until that moment. Some may've referred to it as a downgrade; I'd considered it to be growth. I couldn't ride around in the Caprice forever, especially if I planned to continue striving toward achieving my career goals.

Family Helping Family (2005)

This year was going well. There were no major mishaps for most of the year, and everyone in the family was healthy and trying to enjoy life to the best of their ability. My mom, dad, and Grace were living in a new apartment at Palm Trace Landings in Davie, Florida.

My dad was let go from his job at Tony's Machinery, which wasn't really a bad thing since they were already underpaying him, and he always complained about the fact that they were racist anyway. My dad decided to work for his previous employer's rival, but there was some red tape because he and another coworker, who was also let go, were accused of trying to poach their clientele. Pending an active investigation, including attorneys and investigators, he was out of work for a few months until they were cleared. My dad was a prideful guy who rarely, if ever, asked anyone for favors, but one evening, he called me to help with their rent for a month. I quickly obliged and told him that I would bring him the entire month's rent. Fortunately, I still had a few thousand dollars remaining in my savings account. I'd loan him a good portion so he wouldn't have to worry about where he was going to get the money from.

I just appreciated the fact that I was able to provide something for him when he needed it. I believe it was at that moment that I felt like I stepped into adulthood. The part that got to me the most was that, after he started working again, he had the audacity to tell me he didn't feel like he owed me any money because he considered it a gift. Then, later, he tried to double back and tell me that he would give me a little something once he got into a comfortable position financially. I knew that I wouldn't see a dime when he made that comment, so I refrained from ever asking him about it again. After I gave him the money, I could tell that Monica had certain feelings about it, but she didn't say anything. Her body language said it all. I guess in the back of my mind, I didn't want my dad to get so stressed out about his employment/financial situation that he contemplated going back to his old lifestyle and using drugs again. I know I should've known better, based on my dad's stubborn personality, but there was always a little doubt in the back of my mind that he'd at least think about using again if things got too bad. Thank God he never did.

Attempted Abduction (2005)

On a sunny Wednesday evening, around 5:30 P.M., I received a frantic phone call from Monica, who said that someone had followed her to our parking lot and that I needed to come outside quickly. She started yelling at the person by telling him to get away from her car while he was pounding on her window. I expeditiously hung up the phone, flew off the couch, and sprinted out the front door as fast as I could. I wasn't even fully clothed, except for having on jeans and a wife-beater.

When I got to the parking lot, I saw a stocky black guy with a Polo shirt on pressing his body against the driver's side of her vehicle. He was pulling on the door handle while trying to get into the car.

He kept yelling, "Let me in, let me in, I want to talk to you!"

Monica was yelling and screaming uncontrollably, saying that he was crazy.

I yelled and approached the guy while saying, "Bro, you must be out your damn mind, get away from the car before I beat the brakes off you!"

The guy, with a strong Haitian accent, turned his attention away from the car and glared at me with a menacing look and said, "You want to mess with me, come on, I got AIDS, I got AIDS, come on, come mess with me!"

Before we could physically come into contact with one another, I backpedaled and used Monica's stationary car to distance myself from the man. Monica was still in the vehicle with the doors locked, continuing to scream frantically. I told her to call 911 and keep the doors locked. The guy, realizing that he couldn't get to her, tried to get to me, but I continued to circle the car like a modern-day cat and mouse game. It was all happening so quickly that I couldn't even think clearly.

When I got the opportunity to flee back to the apartment to grab reinforcements and return, he jumped in his car and took off before the police arrived. Monica asked me why I left, and once I showed her the weapon I retrieved from the apartment, she understood what type of timing I was on. About 30 minutes later, the local police finally arrived and filled out a detailed report of what transpired. We called it a night from there and went to bed, both visibly upset after calling our family members and providing vivid details of the dangerous event that took place earlier that evening.

A few days later, while at work, I received a phone call from a detective from the police department stating that he had some pictures he wanted me to look through. When he arrived in the parking lot of my job, we greeted each other, and he pulled out a booklet with photos. We went through 10 to 15 photos, and I finally saw the guy who attempted to attack Monica in one of the pictures. After I identified him as the attacker, the detective thanked me for my time and stated that they would take care of everything from there.

Unexpected Loss (September 11, 2006)

On Monday evening, I received a phone call from Uncle Stetson, who stated that they had found Grandpa Theodore on the bathroom floor, lying face down. I was told that he had a heart attack and died instantly. After speaking with my uncle, I felt numb, as if I had been hit with a ton of bricks.

My grandpa and I may have had our differences from time to time; nevertheless, I still loved him. He was the only grandfather I'd ever known. My dad, who occasionally verbalized to me that he didn't really care for Theodore too much, was even kind of emotional about his death. He did tell me that grandpa was the only father figure he'd ever known, since he'd only spoken to his biological father twice since he was an adult. I was told that when my dad graduated from high school (before leaving for the army), he met up with his biological father and asked him why he didn't sign his birth certificate when he was born. Afterward, he saw him again when he surprisingly showed up at my Great-Grandma Carol's funeral, years ago.

Besides those circumstances, the entire family knew how much Granny loved and cared for Ted; therefore, we knew the grieving process would be difficult for her to deal with on her own. We all took turns looking after and checking in with Granny throughout the week for several months. Eventually, Granny would have to downsize and move into Century Village, which was also in Pembroke Pines, not too far from The Pembroke Lakes Mall. Most of the grandkids pitched in some shape, form, or fashion to help her move by physically assisting with moving her things, and Granny's kids helped both physically and financially.

Turning of the Tide (2007)

After Grandpa Theodore's death, at the start of 2007, I really started to put some things in proper perspective. During that time, my fiancé and I had hit yet another rough patch in our relationship. I made the tough decision to let her know we should break up and go our separate ways. Unfortunately, we were still locked into our lease, so we would have to come up with the additional funds to break it. We agreed to save up enough money over the next few months to get it done.

In the meantime, I would continue to follow my usual routine, which consisted of going to work, coming home, and occasionally visiting with friends, family, and my godson. One day, while visiting my Godson's great-grandparents' house during a family get-together, I was asked about the possibility of becoming a teacher. I had never considered teaching before, even though I'd taken a teaching course as an elective when I was in college years ago. My Godson's great-grandmother worked behind the scenes with the School District of Palm Beach County, and she told me that if I was ever interested in a career change, to let her know. She also said she'd walk me through the steps I would need to take to do so.

I'd take a few weeks to contemplate whether I could try my hand at teaching. I knew that I couldn't be a probation officer forever. Furthermore, I'd grown weary of the same people ending up on probation, violating probation, and going to jail, only to re-offend and get placed on probation all over again eventually. The revolving door associated with my job had become too much for me psychologically. It was rather depressing that there didn't seem to be much I could really do to help people refrain from violating their terms of probation. I figured the best way to become an influential factor in the community was to get into teaching.

After a few phone conversations with my uncle and dad, I decided to accept Mrs. Low's offer and reach out to her about the process of becoming a teacher. She provided me with all the steps that it would take to start the process. I took and passed the 5th through 9th grade English Test as well as the General Knowledge Exam on the first try. Apparently, the General Knowledge Exam was a pretty difficult test to pass, according to many teachers around the district. I was later approved to have a 3-year temporary teaching certificate until I completed the Alternative Certification Program for new teachers who weren't education majors. To receive a permanent teaching certification, I would have to complete the program within the first three years of teaching. Mrs. Low personally set up an interview for me with the principal at JFK Middle School in Riviera Beach.

On the day of the interview, the drive from Boca to Riviera Beach seemed like it took an eternity. My nerves got the best of me to the point where I couldn't even bring myself to turn on the radio. Usually, I'd play some of my favorite rap music to take my mind off things, but that day was different. Physically, I was ready, but mentally I was a wreck. I was dressed in some of my finest professional clothing: black slacks, black Stacey Adams shoes, a black button-up shirt, and a black and white FUBU tie to match. I had a folder with my resume, just in case the principal wanted a hard copy. When I arrived at the school and went through the interview process, I was able to answer all the questions with confidence. When Mr. Green asked me about my background and previous work experience, I shared the trials and tribulations I faced as a youth and my experiences as a current probation officer.

He was intrigued and told me that I would be the right person to work at his school. I was offered the job on the spot, and I kindly accepted. After shaking hands with the principal, I walked back to my car and called Mrs. Low to let her know I got the job as a 7th-grade Language Arts teacher.

Moving on (2007)

After arriving home, I called my family to let them know I would be making a huge career change from probation officer to middle school teacher. Most of them couldn't see me as a teacher. One of my aunts asked me if I was sure I wanted to get into teaching and whether I was ready, based on her previous experiences as a substitute teacher. Of course, I heard all the horror stories that my aunt and uncle had acquired throughout their years of teaching in various classrooms. Still, I also remembered it was a teacher who helped me when I needed it in middle school and who also helped me get off the streets. I felt that everything was finally coming full circle as I became an educator as well.

My next plan of action was to find a place to live not too far from where I would work. I knew I didn't want to live in the same neighborhood as the school, so I decided to look for an apartment in the West Palm area. I remembered hearing all about Riviera Beach on the news every evening before I'd even thought about being interviewed for the position at JFK. The types of crime I heard about in that community reminded me of back home in Miami. I figured that the kids that I'd get would probably be a little rough around the edges, like I was growing up, due to the environment and the potential dynamics of their households. I was psychologically "ready for whatever." Whenever I'd speak to anyone who was originally from the Palm Beach area, and they'd find out where I was going to teach, they would look at me like I was crazy and say, "Good luck."

I ended up finding an apartment with the help of a good friend of mine, Tay, who worked in the reception area of my probation office at the time. Before I officially left that job, I earned the title of Senior Probation Officer, which I was extremely proud of. There were a few added responsibilities that came with the role I was honored to have, such as becoming an official notary for the company and making final decisions on certain pressing situations. The significance of becoming a notary (which the company paid for) was that I was able to sign and notarize documents like violation of probation orders. Even though I enjoyed certain aspects of the role, I knew it was time for me to venture off into another career path.

I officially put in my two weeks' notice at the beginning of July, and I thanked all the higher-ups for the opportunity to work for the company. The director, Maureen, advised me that I could come back at any time, especially if I ended up not liking being a teacher. She also told me that I could return and work during the summer if I was interested. I was shocked by the offer, and I responded by agreeing to return during holiday breaks and during the summer, as long as I was up to it. All of my coworkers wished me luck while simultaneously telling me what to look out for while working in Riviera Beach, as if I didn't grow up on the streets of Miami. The amount of concern and advice they offered was nice since I knew they meant well. All in all, I made some lifelong connections with many of the people I worked with there.

A few weeks later, it was officially moving day for me, at least. The apartment that my former coworker helped me find was a 1-bedroom, 1-bathroom in the Clear Lake Club Apartments on Executive Center Drive. I loved the location because it was inconspicuous and, as the name of the development implied, there was a vast lake in the back. At night, you could look across and see the beautiful city lights of Downtown Clematis. After submitting the application and paying the down payment, I was all set to go.

All I had to do from there was get my stuff and begin the moving process. I rented a U-Haul truck and asked my dad to help me move my belongings from the apartment. As a final goodwill gesture, I packed all of Monica's things for her, even though I wasn't sure when she was moving. I was more concerned with starting a new chapter in my life. The reason why I was so disconnected at that point was because a few weeks back, I found out from Arthur, one of my Miami homeboys from college, that Monica told her friend Mikayla, that she originally wanted to break up with me a while ago because there was a football player she met at Bru's Room that she'd started talking to, behind the scenes. The information really didn't faze me at all, since I'd already moved on. While we were moving my things, Monica tried to enter the apartment and got upset about some of the most trivial things imaginable. I just ignored her as best as I could, but I do remember her stating, "Oh, so you're really serious about this!" You're really leaving? Well, I hope you have a nice life," as she grabbed a few of her things and slammed the door behind her. She shouted that she'd be back for the rest of her stuff once I was gone.

When she left, I gathered the rest of my things and headed from Boca to West Palm to start the next phase of my life. I did have regrets for some of the things that I said and did while Monica and I were together. Still, if there was one thing that I learned that resonated with me more than anything else during our relationship, it was that your significant other isn't your property. Everyone deserves to be loved properly, regardless of the circumstances.

When I finally moved into my new apartment, I was happy and satisfied—finally, a place of my own to call home. The cost of rent for this particular apartment was $800 a month, and I would also be responsible for the water and electricity bills. I quickly made myself at home by arranging everything as I wanted, without interruptions or input from anyone. I officially had a bachelor's pad, although I didn't necessarily remain a bachelor for long. After a few weeks of self-reflection, I realized that I had a fixation for pretty women. It seemed like every other month, I would have another woman in my apartment. Within the first few weeks, I was meeting young ladies everywhere: online, offline, at the store, etc. I'd become a lady magnet somehow, someway. One would've imagined I was like Prince Hakeem from Zamunda (like in the movie "Coming to America"), the way I was sowing my royal oats everywhere. I really had a problem to the point where my front door became a revolving door. At the rate I was going, I was surely heading towards destruction.

My New Career (Aug 2007)

During my first official week of teaching, I was like a fish out of water. It was "pre-school" for all teachers, and the students were due to return the following week. The purpose of "pre-school" was for faculty meetings, professional development trainings, and very minimal time allotted for teachers to work on/in their classrooms. There was so much information and material that was given to us that my head was spinning. I tried to wrap my mind around the fact that I not only had to get my class ready but also had to review and learn the material I was supposed to teach my students. I also had to go through an ESP (The Educator Support Program) and the Alternative Certification Programs to obtain my official teaching certificate. Furthermore, I surely had a lot on my plate, but I was determined to persevere through any obstacles that were in my way.

Most of the teachers that I met that week were cool, and the campus vibe was positive. It was a family atmosphere; everyone welcomed me with open arms, especially after Mr. Green blind-sided me during the latter part of a faculty meeting by stating that I had an interesting story to tell about my upbringing. Begrudgingly, I provided the staff with an overview of my upbringing and how I overcame challenges with the help of my uncle. There wasn't a dry eye in the room. I was extremely nervous since that was the first time actually telling an entire crowd of strangers what I went through. Many staff members thanked me for being vulnerable and for inspiring them to be mindful of the fact that the kids at our school come from diverse backgrounds and environments. To be honest, after I finished speaking in front of everyone, I felt empowered. I had my doubts about being as transparent as I was. The next idea that ran across my mind was, "Maybe I should speak about my experiences more often, especially if it affects people this way?"

At the conclusion of the meeting, I was assigned a mentor teacher named Mr. Beach. Mr. Beach was also a language arts teacher who had over twenty years of experience. He recommended that I obtain certain essential materials for my students, seeing that many of them were coming from adverse situations at home. I was given a bunch of pencils, pens, notebook paper, and a case of copy paper. Mr. Beach also told me that I would have to be firm because the students would "try" me since I am a brand-new teacher. When he told me that, I started to formulate a plan. I figured that I'd use my previous experiences of growing up in the inner city and working as a probation officer to spark the student's interest in my story of perseverance. I knew that to acquire their respect, I would have to be as relatable as possible.

Toward the end of the week, my principal told me that I would be one of the five male teachers handpicked to teach in the school's "Boyz 2 Men" program. This program involved taking 7th-grade boys, who were in the bottom twenty-five percent in reading and math, and placing them on a strict schedule where they remained in the same classes together throughout the day. They would have only the strongest male teachers in each class, and social skills development would be incorporated into the curriculum as well. The possible incentives they could earn for meeting the behavior expectations of the program included field trips to various places, among other activities.

223

***

My first week with the students was smooth at first, until I started seeing little mischievous behaviors as each day passed. I could tell that some of my classes were going to be softer than others based on the wide array of personalities I had to deal with. During the honeymoon phase, most of my classes were cool, especially after I shared how I grew up and what my former occupation was. They were so inquisitive and appreciative of the fact that I told them about my experiences. Some of my students stated that they could relate to some of the things I went through, while others quickly told me that their relatives were either currently or at one time on probation or in prison. At times, the conversations got out of hand, but for the most part, I accomplished my initial goal of becoming relatable in their eyes.

Within my first few months of teaching, tragedy struck. One of the popular students throughout the campus, Len, was hit by a train in October. Details about the incident remained unclear, though rumors suggested she was with a group of friends playing around near the tracks. Another rumor circulating in the community was that she was accidentally pushed by one of her friends. In any event, it was a tremendously somber moment on campus. While many of the students were visibly upset, some seemed to be unbothered by it. Apparently, that wasn't an uncommon occurrence within the community; some of the kids were numb to it. A few of my coworkers informed me that many unfortunate events in the "Da Raw," as they often referred to Riviera Beach, usually were the result of gang or domestic violence. From that point on, I knew I had my work cut out for me because the kids at our school faced many challenges outside of academics, which I totally understood.

Strategic Moves (2007)

The problems developed when many of my students started acting out to get my attention. Initially, I didn't understand it. After a while, I could tell they were competing to prove who was the toughest. If I had one class all day long, it would've been easy to manage, but five periods of the same issues every day was a bit much for any mere mortal such as myself. I attributed their craving for my attention to their craving for attention, but I never verbalized that to them. My methods of attempting to shut down misbehavior as swiftly and as aggressively as possible were unsuccessful at times. My approach of combining my upbringing in the streets of Miami with my background in the criminal justice system led to more issues than resolutions. Unfortunately, many of my antics encouraged my students in several of my classes to revolt against my rules and behavioral expectations.

From the end of August to October was pure hell on earth for me, as well as some of my students. Regardless, I wasn't about to back down, nor were they. There were many verbal sparring matches and a few heated moments that would've led to physical altercations if things had persisted. I was truly at my wit's end, until I checked myself one day, and realized that the problem wasn't the students; in actuality, it was me. I completely lost sight of my purpose for getting into education because I would feel some way when the boys said or did things that disrespected me. I had to take my personal feelings out of the equation and ask myself, "Am I the type of teacher I would've been able to talk to or rely on when I was going through my personal turmoil on the streets? The short and simple answer was "No."

225

Finally, I decided to try a new approach. I knew I had to go back to the drawing board. I asked one of my students for his youth football schedule for the remainder of their season. I would hear that in "Da Raw," the youth football games at Tate's Field were the place to be on Saturdays. I wanted to go out there and support some of my students, to show them they were more important to me than test scores and letter grades. When I got there, I saw some of everybody: a couple of coworkers, many of my students from school, their families, and one or two of my homeboys from college who were either coaching or watching the nephews or cousins play.

The atmosphere around the park reminded me of back home in Miami. There was a DJ playing music, and little kids (who weren't football players) were running around, playing, laughing, and socializing. It felt like a home away from home. Once some of the kids from JFK spotted me, they couldn't believe it. I could feel all the eyes staring at me as I strolled around the park, using my superhero-like peripheral vision to spot some of the parents of my students whom I remembered meeting during open house earlier in the year. I was kind of surprised that I was spotted so easily since I wasn't in my normal "Church clothes" (as the kids loved to call them).

My students would always ask me why I dressed up every day, and I would respond that I wanted to be a good example for them. I'd often tell my students things such as, "You don't have to wait until you go to church, a club, or a special event to dress nicely." The boys would laugh and say, "Mr. Lennon thinks he's fresh, but he do be matching though!" I'd commonly wear a variety of button-up shirts, slacks, ties, and colored shoes that matched the rest of my outfit. Monday through Friday, I was always "casket-sharp." At the park that day, I wore black and white Jordan 1s, black Jordan basketball shorts with matching socks, a white t-shirt, some jewelry, and a black 305 fitted hat. I didn't think I had anything flashy or special on, but the kids who saw me seemed both impressed and surprised. I stayed and watched two games back-to-back, conversing and introducing myself to many of the parents and coaches who were there, but only when the opportunity presented itself.

Many of the students were happy to see me, but the notoriously mischievous ones in class tried to dodge me like the plague. I made it a point to find them after their games to discover who their parents or guardians were and where they lived, so I could conveniently introduce myself. I'd avoid talking about the particulars of my class at the time, I just wanted the students to know that I was vested in their well-being, to the point that I'd go to unconventional lengths to reach their loved ones, if I needed to.

***

When the weekend ended and the kids returned to school, a mob of them swarmed my door threshold that Monday morning. Most of them I knew, some I didn't. They asked me a million and one questions about last Saturday at Tate's. I guess it was a thing because I was constantly asked about it all day long. When word spread throughout the campus, other kids started asking me if I would come to their games or events. Part of me was honored, but another part of me was saddened to know that these poor kids all wanted the same thing: attention and support from someone who truly cares. I would do my due diligence to attend different events throughout the community.

That week, I noticed a noticeable change in my students' behavior, and in return, I continued to make a positive adjustment in my approach with them. I actually aimed to listen when they needed to express themselves. Gradually, that mutual respect was established because the kids could tell that I genuinely cared about them as individuals. From that point on, I became one of the "go-to" teachers for my students when they needed advice or wanted to vent about something.

Church in The Raw (2007)

Mr. Dale, who was one of the teachers I quickly became friends with at JFK, invited me to his church in the heart of Riviera Beach. I figured I might as well give it a try since I was a bit overdue for finding a church home in Palm Beach.

When I got there, I noticed the church had a classic "old school" feel, which I enjoyed. It reminded me of my family's church home back in Miami. The Pastor was a middle-aged, energetic fellow named Reverend Teddy, who had a knack for delivering the word in a manner that appealed to everyone. The members of the church embraced me with open arms, and I became a frequent attendee. I even started bringing some of the students whom I mentored on Sunday mornings. Now and then, I'd even take the entire crew to the Southern Kitchen buffet in North Lake before dropping them off at home. I just hoped they were aware that it was through the grace of God that I was able to be in the position to look out for them when I could. I remember what it was like to feel hopeless and want to give up based on my circumstances while growing up. All of their parents were appreciative of the support, and I think those experiences were healing for me as well.

Having the ability to give back in a way that was somewhat similar, but not as severe as what my uncle did for me, was all the thanks I really needed. In hindsight, I was yearning for a family of my own, but until I could find the right woman to marry and start having children with, I decided to give one hundred and ten percent into mentoring some of the misunderstood youth in "Da Raw."

Emergency Call (2007)

At 10 P.M., on a Friday night, an unexpected phone call woke me out of my sleep. It was Oscar, one of my mentees. He apologized for calling so late and stated he didn't know where else to turn for help. He told me his mom's check from didn't hit her account, and they didn't have anything to eat at their house. He also mentioned that he and his two brothers were hungry and wondered if there was anything I could do to help. His mother was currently working the overnight shift at a medical facility, about 20 minutes away.

I told him, "No problem," as I got dressed and drove to the 24-hour Walmart on Congress Avenue to purchase food for the boys.

Initially, I intended to get a few items to hold them over for the night. Still, before I knew it, I was going down just about every aisle, grabbing stuff that I assumed they'd like from cereal, milk, pre-made frozen chicken dinners, hamburger helper, cheese, deli meat, juice, water, etc. When I finally made it to the cash register, there was $200 worth of food in my cart. When I saw the total, I didn't flinch. One thing was for certain, two things for sure; I wasn't about to let kids go hungry, and I wasn't going to let anyone down, especially if they were depending on me.

After leaving Walmart and arriving at the boys' house to drop off the groceries, they were already outside patiently waiting. Oscar timidly said, "My bad, Mr. Lennon, I know it's late!" I told him, "No worries, this was an emergency." He and his brothers were advised to grab the bags out of the trunk after I told them,

"This ain't no delivery service, get to work," trying to make light of the situation.

After they obtained all the groceries from my car, they thanked me, and I gave each of them dap before driving back home for some much-deserved sleep. That for sure wouldn't be the last time I'd look out for one of my mentees' well-being, especially when it came to helping with food or a late light bill or two.

Assistant Coaching (2007)

During my first year of teaching, I quickly found out that one of the most influential people on campus was Coach Mitch. He was about twenty-five years older than I was, and he was a hometown hero. The kids at the school and throughout the community loved him. Mitch was a behavior interventionist who worked in the EBD (emotional and behavioral disorders) unit. He had an uncanny skill for reaching students in special education because he knew most of their families, having grown up in the area himself.

When Mitch and I met, we quickly became friends because we shared some of the same interests: we were both avid sports fans, and we had a strong desire to see all kids make it out of their environment. Coach Mitch was a former college football player who decided to return to his hometown to raise his family. Before he got into education, he worked for Florida Power and Light for many years. When he transitioned to work for the Palm Beach County School District, he coached football at Suncoast High as well as the boys' basketball at JFK. He'd often tell me all about the many middle school championships his teams won over the years and the heated rivalry they had with Roosevelt Middle. He asked me if I wanted to coach with him, and I didn't hesitate to jump at the chance.

Before that time, I never considered trying my hand at coaching, but I figured that since I've played, trained, and watched the sport long enough, I could potentially help here and there. After the first practice, I could see it wasn't a "help out whenever I feel like it" position. Everything from the tryouts to the practices was intense. While many of the student-athletes were rough around the edges and undisciplined, I knew Mitch would whip them into shape. I surely enjoyed helping with basketball, but I also appreciated that we were indirectly preparing them for life as a whole. Between Mitch's and my life experiences, we had a lot to offer the boys we coached.

My first season coaching with Mitch was great, even though it took some time getting adjusted to how he generally did things. Not only was he the head basketball coach, but he was also the bus driver for all away-game sporting events. He had a lot on his plate. From time to time, I'd run a practice or two if he had a scheduling conflict. The regular season didn't go as planned. We ended with a subpar 6-5 record, even though we had a few really talented players. After the first few games of the season, we knew the team wasn't going to compete with the top teams in the division because we only had a starting five that could really hoop for real. We also had two players who were ineligible to play due to their poor grades and terrible behavior in school.

***

After the disappointing basketball season ended, it was time to focus on preparing my students for the annual writing and reading portions of the FCAT. It was like pulling teeth trying to get them motivated to test. With the death of one of their most influential schoolmates, the students didn't really care about testing, and I couldn't blame them. Truth be told, I couldn't care less about the test either, but I couldn't let the kids know that. Instead of pushing the issue, I would do what I could academically and try to support all the kids struggling to cope with everything that transpired over the past few months. I would allow them to have "real-talk" conversations with me.

That tactic created a safe space for them to express themselves without fearing judgment based on what they had to say, no matter how they said it. Even though our school fared horribly during the statewide testing, at least my students felt empowered and respected during that tumultuous time in their lives. Who knows, some of the verbal jewels I was able to drop on them may have been key to saving some of their lives, outside of school.

Unexpected Death (2008)

Toward the latter part of April, I received a call from Mitch that devastated me. I'd never heard him so upset before. He told me that Ervin, one of our 8th-grade basketball players, died that evening. The story he was told was when Ervin was walking his dog behind the complex where he lived, right along the tracks, he didn't notice a train was coming because he had headphones on at the time. His dog ran across the tracks, and when he went to retrieve him, the train struck him.

The news struck a chord with me because that same day, when school ended, Ervin called my cell phone and asked if I could give him a ride home. I told him I couldn't because I had an appointment immediately after school. As I was telling Mitch about it, I felt guilty, and I started thinking whether or not his death could've been prevented if I had just given him a ride home that day. Maybe he would've held off on walking his dog after I dropped him off. I never told anyone but Mitch about the guilt I felt, so I just kept it to myself.

Due to his overwhelming popularity across campus, it was decided that the funeral service would be held in our school's gymnasium. Reverend Masters was summoned to perform the eulogy. It was a heart-wrenching service, and all everyone could talk about was how much Ervin loved basketball and cracking jokes. One of his 7th-grade teammates, Mark, mentioned that he and Mal received a special message after our playoff loss to Jupiter Middle earlier that year.

He stated to them, "Aye, lil bro's make sure y'all win it all for me next year!"

Recognition (2008)

During our end-of-the-year faculty meeting, our principal gave out a few awards to the non-instructional and instructional staff members who were felt to have gone above and beyond for their students and/or our colleagues.

To my surprise, I was awarded the "New Teacher of the Year Award" for the 2007-2008 school year. That totally took me by surprise because some awesome teachers were also in their first year of teaching. What probably put me over the top was all the work I was putting in behind the scenes in the community. When I went up to accept my award in front of the entire faculty and staff, I thanked everyone for their help and guidance during the year.

After the meeting was over, we all ate and fellowshipped a bit. The majority of my coworkers congratulated me and told me, "Don't worry about the trials and errors that took place that year; as the years go by, and you gain more experience, things will get easier." I took heed to the advice and words of encouragement, but I had a hard time imagining things going easier in a profession that was deemed a second career.

To me personally, while I came a long way with improving my classroom management skills, I felt as if I left a lot to be desired regarding academic enrichment. I know I could've been better prepared to deliver the curriculum more effectively if I had been given adequate time to prepare. It seemed as if I was basically handed the keys to the classroom, with a few materials in hand, and told to give it my best shot.

After the school year ended, I took a few weeks to reflect on all the events that took place. I decided to spend part of my summer studying the curriculum to ensure my future students would have what they needed to succeed by the time the annual Florida Comprehensive Assessment Test rolled around.

My Second Year (2008-2009)

My second year of teaching was much smoother than the year before. This year, I would have traditional co-ed classes every period. I was starting to acquire quite a reputation in the community for my efforts with St. Jones Church and the students whom I was mentoring. From what I heard, word got around that I didn't play games in the classroom, either.

Unlike my first year of teaching, I began by getting to know my students and allowing them to get to know me. This approach paid dividends and helped me avoid some of the issues I faced during my first year. My biggest issue at the beginning of the year was students coming to class without the materials they needed every day. After the first two weeks of school, I decided that I'd nip the issue in the bud before things could really get out of hand. One day after work, I went to Big Lots and purchased over 120 college-ruled notebooks for my students. Thankfully, the store still had an assortment of notebooks from their "Back to School" sale. I was able to get them for fifteen cents apiece, so I decided to purchase a bunch of pencils as well.

The next day, as I presented the notebooks to each of my five class periods, most of my students were very appreciative that I went out of my way to purchase materials for them with my own money. I told them, "In my class, failure was not an option, and the first way to set yourselves up for success was to be prepared at all times." Afterward, I informed them that they would not be allowed to take the notebooks out of the room unless I authorized them to do so. Of course, they asked me why; I just told them that I didn't trust them to actually bring the notebooks back and forth from

239

home every day. They understood and agreed to keep the notebooks in a designated spot on the counter in my room.

Between telling them about my upbringing and providing them with materials that many of them needed, all of my students knew that I was a little different from the teachers they were used to.

***

My second season as the assistant coach of the basketball team started off more productively than the year before. Mitch and I were determined to return JFK basketball to prominence. We started off that year with intramural basketball, which was sort of like open gym sessions, so we could get an early look at the type of talent we had coming in.

We already knew we had a few impactful returners from the previous year, such as Mal and Mark. Mitch told me that we also had a few transfer students coming from a few of the local schools in the area. Deebo, Ted, and Clinton were the most impactful transfers. Deebo was an athletic ball of energy, with the speed of Sonic the Hedgehog but an inconsistent jump shot; Ted was a physical bully on the court, who had a silky mid-range jump shot, and Clinton was as athletic as Deebo, but he could do a little of everything on the court. With those three, we knew we could whip them into shape with discipline and consistency. We also had incoming sixth grader Q, who was very talented but small and unassuming. Q's mother was a current science teacher at the school, and we knew he probably wouldn't be much of a factor that year. Ted and Deebo tortured him on a daily basis while in practice.

The two of them were overly physical with him, and the excuse they made for it was that they were making him tougher for next year. Q hated the experience so much that he contemplated quitting, but Mitch and I kept him encouraged. As for the progress of the season, everything went according to plan. We went undefeated and made it to the county championship to face Lake Worth Middle in our gym. The first half of the game was horrible for us; we were outplayed in every aspect of the game. They were the bigger team, and they looked intimidating. A few of their players had mustaches, goatees, and long dreadlocks; we just knew that some of them were older than the average middle schooler. Going into the locker room at the half, we didn't make any excuses for their poor play, as Mitch gave them a passionate speech about playing with pride. I shared a few words with the team afterward, but I could tell I didn't need to say much because Mitch's message was loud and clear. When the third quarter started, both teams took a while to get cooking on the offensive end, but defensively, the same intensity from the first half carried over.

At the start of the fourth quarter, we were down by double digits, and that's when the "Deebo Effect" came into play. He led the frantic charge that got us back into the game. First, he got a key steal and an uncharacteristic three-pointer. Then he blocked a dunk attempt that led to a layup on the other end. Those two sequences were just enough to get the rest of the team going. Before we knew it, Mal, Ted, and Clinton started scoring to the point where we went up by five points. Mitch and I couldn't do anything but look at each other, smile, and agree that "These boys were playing some basketball now!" When the game clock expired, we completed a phenomenal comeback victory that no one in the gym expected. Everyone rushed to the court and celebrated hysterically. It was like a scene out of a movie. After all the hoopla on the court, we went into the locker room and celebrated a little more. Mal and Mark both elaborated that "this championship was for Ervin."

Ingratiated in the Word (2009)

After basketball season ended, I dedicated more time, energy, and effort to reading and understanding the word of God. I would get more in tune with scripture by not only reading it, but also studying it. Although I did struggle with understanding certain concepts and terminology, I was able to seek the guidance of a few friends I made at church (Precious and Jay).

They were sort of like my spiritual brothers and sisters. Jay taught me the importance of having access to a concordance while reading the Bible. Concordances served as a quick and easy way of searching for the meaning of specific words or phrases and the identification of patterns or themes within the text. They really came in handy, considering there were many terms and phrases that were difficult for me to understand when I first started really attempting to study the Bible.

Aside from them, there were many stellar examples of how to be positive models for the youth in the community, such as Terence and his father. They were the epitome of stewards of their community. From driving kids to and from church on Sundays to mentoring and encouraging them to attend Bible study sessions, they did it all. After a while, I would feel the courage to let the pastor as well as the members of the congregation know about my humble beginnings and how I was able to overcome the situations I experienced growing up. The more I opened up and let people know more about who I was as a person, the more they gravitated toward me. Many of the members of the church often said I seemed as if I always had a smile on my face. The truth was, since

I spent so many years of my childhood surrounded by negativity, I subconsciously made a vow to try to be as positive as possible.

At the beginning of August, during an event at the church, Pastor Teddy asked me if I could meet him in his office to talk about something important. When I got there, he took a seat behind his desk and started telling me how impressed he was with how quickly everyone was gravitating towards me since I started attending church there. He also asked me how I would feel about delivering a "Back to School" message for the parents and kids of the church the following Sunday. Initially, I was a little apprehensive due to my lack of experience in public speaking. After a few seconds of gathering my thoughts, I said to myself, "Who am I to say no to a man of the cloth?" So, after careful deliberation, I agreed to do the "Sermonette" next Sunday.

When I left his office, I let Precious, Jay, and another friend from the church named Tiff know that I needed a little help with scriptures to use as reference points for my upcoming speech. They were, by all means, a great help, and some of the concepts that I decided to talk about were salvation, people playing church, deception, and the dangers of lukewarm behaviors. I was able to incorporate a great deal of my personal experiences into the methodically planned speech I wrote. I went from semi-confident to an unusual boldness in the messages that I planned to deliver. As a matter of fact, I was so confident that I invited my dad, my sister, and Granny to St. Jones to attend the service.

When Sunday came, I was extremely nervous but well-prepared. I had an index card with all the key points that I wanted to address written on it in order to ensure that I wouldn't forget anything. When it was time for me to speak, the pastor gave me a fitting introduction as I stepped into the pulpit. After greeting the congregation and visitors, I started my message as planned, but something came over me as I got into the meat of what I intended to say. It felt like an out-of-body experience, because I could hear words coming out of my mouth, although I didn't know where they were coming from. Some of the things that I wanted to touch upon were lightly addressed; I guess God had different plans for me and my message that morning. It would be the first, yet certainly not the last time, having the Holy Spirit take over and speak through me.

After I concluded my message, everyone clapped as I sat down, and the pastor proceeded to deliver his sermon. Oddly enough, he would surprisingly contradict parts of my message. Earlier in my message to the parents, I attempted to encourage them to put their best efforts into providing their kids with an example of how to resist the temptation to sin. When the pastor started saying things such as "Nobody's perfect" and "We are all sinners" (which are all true), I didn't know where he was headed with his sermon until he provided a surprising example. The pastor mentioned the singer Beyoncé and how she gyrates on stages when she performs. He also proceeded to comment on how good she looked while performing, and I immediately started squirming in my seat.

Spiritually, something felt odd about his statements. The last straw was when he made a failed attempt at manipulating scripture to justify his statements. I couldn't help but look into the crowd, and when I saw Precious, Jay, and a few other faces, I could see the disgust. If I weren't sitting in the pulpit, I'm pretty sure I would have had the same look on my face as well. That was the moment that I realized that particular sanctuary wasn't the place for me anymore. After the service concluded, I met my family members outside the church. Each one of them congratulated me for a job well done. When I got to my friends Precious, Jay, and Tiff, they looked at me, greeted me, and said, "You know we gotta talk, right?" I responded by saying, "Yeah, I already know," with a look of disgust on my face.

After the service, as my family drove back down south, I returned to my apartment to take a quick shower in preparation to go to Precious and Jay's apartment to talk about how things played out at St. Jones. Once I got there, we all looked at each other and yelled to the top of our lungs, "What in the world was Pastor talking about!" They told me how it was "messed up" that the pastor contradicted my message like that. Precious said that she was so ashamed that the majority of the congregation was clapping and co-signing his sermon, even though it was apparent that it wasn't spirit-led. That evening, I learned a lot of information from them about the dynamics of the congregation at St. Jones. After getting caught up to speed on the inner workings of our church, I told my friends that I'd never set foot in that place ever again.

Another Championship (2010-2011)

Last season ended with a heartbreaking playoff defeat to Roosevelt Middle. We had an opportunity to push the game into overtime with a last-second shot attempt at the end of regulation, but Ted couldn't make the highly contested mid-range jumper.

In the upcoming year, we knew things would be very different. Q was an 8th grader, and he'd gotten much taller, slimmer, faster, and more aggressive than ever before. Mitch said that we would go as far as Q, and Lester would carry us. Lester was tall and quiet but pretty skilled as well, for a "youngin." We pretty much ran through our regular season schedule without a hiccup. Between our full-court press and the overload offense, we were the favorites to win the county championship that year. The only team we would have to get through to reach the championship was Roosevelt, as usual. We played them at home to decide who would make it to the big game. The word on the street was that Roosevelt was supposed to pull up and blow our team out from the beginning to the end.

To put it mildly, the game didn't go the way they planned it to. Before it started, I used the alleged trash talk as motivation for our team. Of course, I put my own spin on what was allegedly said to get a rise out of Q and the rest of our hoopers. Good thing it worked, because part of me felt a certain way about stretching the truth a bit. All in all, we beat the brakes off of Roosevelt from the beginning of the second half to the end of the game. The first half was extremely chippy between their team and ours. Every time the opposition would attempt to make a run, Q would impose his will on both the offensive and defensive ends of the court. If he wasn't knocking down timely three-pointers or getting steals, he was slicing and dicing his way to the hoop for contested layups.

In the fourth quarter, we were able to let our less experienced 6th graders play the majority of the 4th quarter. After the game, we let the kids celebrate a little, but they knew that the job wasn't done until we won the championship. Our opponent during the championship game the following week was Carver Middle. The matchup was rumored to be huge because Carver had an 8th-grade point guard named Jamal, who people felt was just as good as Q. We knew that Q was going to give it his all to win and prove he was the best 8th grader in the county. During the championship game at our gym, Q and Jamal were going at it, but Q proved to be too much for him. He was out there like a man possessed. Q was all over the place, diving for loose balls, wreaking havoc on defense, and also leading the offensive charge.

In the end, we were able to pull out a solid victory and win our second championship in 4 years. After the game, we were presented with the county championship trophy, and we took a few team photos. A representative from the Palm Beach Post even interviewed coach Mitch and Q.

Something New (2011-2012)

As the new school year started, I found myself overextending my generous deeds to any and every kid who needed guidance. I went from mentoring a few select students to mentoring seven kids/teens, both males and females. Some of them moved on to high school, and others were in middle school.

It was as if I were trying to save the world, one group of kids at a time, since I started teaching at Kennedy. I loved that I was able to become the person I would've wanted to be a part of my life when I was going through my trials and tribulations as a kid. Suppose I wasn't attending their sporting events, birthday celebrations, and acting as an occasional chauffeur. In that case, I was giving advice or lending a listening ear so they could vent about their problems. All in all, I would always try to incorporate messages about God in whatever advice I'd give them.

I would have to slowly disassociate myself from some of my mentees and their families after realizing that they were taking advantage of my efforts to be a positive light in their lives. For instance, one evening I received a particular phone call from Oscar stating that his mom was short on the bills, and she needed a hundred and fifty dollars for the light bill.

I was skeptical about the situation from the jump, but I decided to help them out one last time and then distance myself from them afterward. It was a hard decision to make, but a wise person once told me that I was "doing too much" by serving as a crutch for those whom I thought I was helping. It seemed as if I was fulfilling the role of their own personal savior, which wasn't my intention.

That message hit home, and I'd start to focus a little more on myself than others.

Before I knew it, by having so much free time to "do me," I'd become a serial dater again. Every few months, I would engage in new relationships and "situationships" that led nowhere. Then, in January 2011, I met someone special named Donna. She was one of the prettiest, most well-reserved women that I've come across in a long time. She was a woman of faith who had a stable career in nursing. The only catch was that she had a five-year-old daughter named Netta from a previous marriage. My reservations about her having a child pertained to the previous vow I made to myself when I was in college, not to get seriously involved with any more women who had children. With how nice, beautiful, and intriguing Donna seemed, I decided to take a chance and wholeheartedly pursue a relationship with her.

One of the things I respected the most about her was her reluctance to allow me to meet Netta until we were in a serious relationship. I loved how cautious she was, and I completely understood why. When I finally met her daughter, she was a little shy at first, then, before I knew it, she warmed up to me when she felt comfortable enough to do so.

After a month, I would start going down to Donna's apartment to spend time with her every weekend. I'd get off work at 4 P.M. on Friday and head straight to my apartment to grab clothes for the next few days. Afterward, I would routinely drive down I-95 to head south for Pembroke Pines. That would become a weekly routine. After a while, I would also spend time building a bond with Netta by taking her to the "Playmobil Fun Park" in Palm Beach Gardens. We'd also go to the local park so she could swing on the swing set, among other fun activities. Now, the unique thing about the Playmobil Fun Park was its distinctiveness. It was truly a little kid's dream, with unlimited amounts of Legos and action figures to play with. They even had different themes throughout the establishment that went along with particular types of Legos. It was definitely a sight to see for Netta. As for me, I was totally overstimulated, though I kept a poker face on to avoid spoiling Netta's ability to have the time of her life. We spent about an hour there, and then headed to "Menchies," a frozen yogurt spot, to grab ice cream before heading back down south.

As a nurse, Donna's work schedule consisted of working three 12-hour shifts during the week; she also worked every other weekend. On those Fridays, I would eventually start driving down to pick up Netta from school. During those weekends, I'd take care of her at Donna's apartment instead of her dropping her off at her parent's house, like she used to do before we met. Netta had never met her biological father due to particular unsafe circumstances Donna told me about. After I found out what transpired when she was a baby, I was determined to fill the void of Netta not having a father figure in her life.

I told Donna I would ensure both of them were as happy and well taken care of. It wouldn't be long before I started teaching Netta little things I felt would be good for her at her current age, such as the importance of not throwing away food, how to vacuum, and how to perform cartwheels (with the help of YouTube, of course). Once she got the cartwheels down, I was able to convince Donna to sign her up for gymnastics. To everyone's surprise, she was an instant hit. She caught on quickly, and it seemed as if she was on her way to becoming a dynamic little gymnast. I was so proud of her. The same little girl I taught how to do a basic cartwheel off the edge of her mother's couch was actually in weekend gymnastics classes, thriving. All was right in the world at this point; work was going well, Donna and I quickly fell in love, and everywhere I went, my shadow, Netta, was with me.

In April, I decided I didn't want to waste any more time dating Donna, as I knew she was the woman I wanted to spend the rest of my life with. I would take a few thousand dollars from my savings account and put it towards a near-perfect diamond wedding/engagement set from Zale's, that was fit for a queen. I thought about how her father would possibly react when I'd go ask him for his blessing to propose to his daughter, and the thought of doing so scared me, to be honest, but I didn't let it deter me.

After picking out the elegant rings, I ventured over to Donna's parents' house to have the dreaded conversation with her pops. When I asked if we could speak in private, he walked me over to his man cave (garage), and I proceeded to tell him, "even though I realized that it had been a short amount of time," I was in love with Donna, and I wanted his blessing to propose to her. He smiled and asked me if I was sure, which was particularly funny to me. It felt as if it were some pre-warning he was subliminally trying to give me. Afterward, he told me he respected how I came to him, asked for his permission, and said he'd be honored to welcome me into the family. We shook hands and gave each other a quick hug. He then started to tell me how he noticed how quickly Netta gravitated towards me from the start.

He also told me, "Whatever you do, take care of my girls and protect them at all costs."

I told him, "No problem."

Within the next month, I planned to propose to Donna in such a unique way that she would remember it for the rest of her life. Netta was spending time at Donna's parents' house, and Donna and I drove to Walmart to pick up some things for her apartment.

When we parked and were getting ready to get out of the car, I told her I couldn't find my wallet. I pretended to look through the front seat of the car while she was on the passenger side looking as well, but I had already covertly obtained the ring from under my seat. I got out of the car as if I was frantic about my missing wallet, made my way to the passenger-side door, and opened it.

Donna looked at me as if to say, "What are you doing?"

I squatted down as if I was about to tie my shoe, and I got down on one knee and proposed. Donna couldn't believe it, and she quickly said, "Yes," with much excitement and confusion. She said the proposal was totally unexpected. We both knew everyone would feel we were moving too fast. We loved each other, and we wanted to be together for the rest of our lives, so whatever the naysayers thought didn't matter to us. We would set the wedding date for June 2012.

Getting Things Situated (2012)

As our wedding day quickly approached, there were many different things taking place all around us. As expected, my father told me he was splitting up with my mom.

A week later, Donna and I helped him move out of their apartment to Century Village with Granny. On top of that, Donna, Netta, and I had recently moved into our own apartment a month before our wedding date. I wasn't initially opposed to moving down to Broward County from Palm Beach, but Donna was adamant that she and Netta move close to where I resided. We settled on renting a quaint, 2-bedroom, 2-bathroom apartment in Boynton Beach. Thankfully, there was a great elementary school around the corner, and we enrolled Netta in it just before school started.

The troublesome situation I also had to come to grips with at the time was dealing with my father's deteriorating mental health. When I would talk to him on the phone, he'd often repeat himself and forget about some of the previous parts of the conversation we'd had. The rest of my family and I noticed something was seriously off with him, but none of us could put a finger on what it might've been.

Wedding Day (Jun 2012)

On our wedding day, I was so incredibly nervous that I couldn't keep myself together. I was sweating profusely, and I couldn't stop pacing back and forth. My dad, Donna's father, and I all took pictures before the actual wedding ceremony, which was a cool experience.

We didn't have a huge, extravagant wedding, but we did have fifty to seventy-five of our relatives and close friends there. During the wedding, as Donna was escorted down the aisle by her father, I was so excited to finally marry the woman of my dreams. I kept thinking to myself, "God, please don't let anything go wrong right now." My coworker, Mr. Dale, was the person who was there to marry us.

As Donna and I read our vows and exchanged rings, I felt the happiest I'd ever been in my life. After saying, "We do," and embracing, I hugged Netta as we made our way to the reception area, which was also conveniently located at the venue. We all danced, ate, and enjoyed ourselves for the rest of the evening.

A Blessing from God (Jul 2012)

A month after our wedding, Donna and I discovered she was pregnant sometime at the end of July. We were all elated because it was our plan to get pregnant as soon as possible after our wedding. As we announced the pregnancy to the world via social media and in person to our family and friends, everyone was excited for us. As Donna continued to work her three 12-hour shifts, I would intentionally pick up the slack in all facets of our household. I didn't want her to endure any unnecessary stress that would potentially put her or our baby's health at risk.

As far as Netta was concerned, I would spend a lot of time ensuring she was prepared for her first year of public school. I knew the first thing I'd have to do was make sure her reading skills were up to par. I'd use the strategies I acquired from teaching to make sure she was ahead of the game once school started. Furthermore, I purchased blank, white index cards and wrote basic sight words on them. The purpose of the index cards was to improve her spelling ability. I even went as far as creating index cards for the objects around the apartment and taping them on each item. I was determined to see her thrive, so I'd quiz her daily until she got each one correct.

Afterward, I'd take her to the Boynton Beach library to show her how to correctly preview and check out books. The first day I took her there, she ended up checking out five age-appropriate books that she read within 24 hours of receiving them. Donna and I were shocked that she read them so fast that when I took her back the next weekend, she checked out twelve more books. She ecstatically stated, "Can I really check out all these books? Yay!"

She was the happiest I've seen her since Donna and I got together. Netta was a reading wizard who enjoyed picking out stories she was interested in. This was encouraging to see since I understood how important literacy was.

When the new school year started, I was terribly nervous. I wasn't nervous about my job or anything; I was worried about Netta adjusting to school in a new county. It was her first year in public school as well. I'd grown so protective of her that I wanted to do anything and everything to keep her safe. The unknown of how she would adapt to a new environment, whether she'd grasp the content academically, and if she would be prone to being bullied were just a few of the things I was highly concerned about.

Most of the week, I would take her to school in the mornings before driving to Riviera Beach for work. On the first day of school, as I dropped her off, I felt like a defenseless parent watching her get out of the car and walk into the school for the first time. As the year progressed, we all developed a great routine that worked for us. Donna and I utilized teamwork to take turns picking up Netta from school until it was time for basketball season to start. I definitely enjoyed having her as a riding partner, especially in the mornings. We'd sing and dance along to the latest gospel rap songs I compiled on my SoundCloud playlist. As soon as we got into my car, and I connected my phone to the Bluetooth of my stereo, Netta would smile and start singing along since she had memorized my playlist.

From August to December, everything went as smoothly as possible. During that time, Netta made friends in school, and she even attended gymnastics classes at Genie's Gymnastics. Donna's belly had gotten larger with every passing day, and I was extremely exhausted but happy that everyone was doing well. Our first Christmas as a married couple was nearly perfect. I prepared a feast fit for 6 to 8 people, though it was only the 3 of us. Netta received a gang of presents from both sides of our family. Though Donna and I exchanged a few gifts, we were more than content with the greatest gift we could offer one another, our bundle of joy, who was on the way soon.

Complications (Jan 2013)

During the middle of January, Donna began to have stomach discomfort, and we were extremely concerned that there were potential complications with her pregnancy. We would make frequent visits from our apartment in Boynton Beach to the hospital in Pembroke Pines to ensure things were going well. We didn't want to take any chances. We would take the long drive because Donna only felt comfortable with the hospital where she worked. Both of us were undoubtedly firm believers of the saying, "Better safe than sorry."

One evening, she started having constant contractions, and we drove back down south only to be told it was a false alarm. After a long night at the hospital, as we arrived back home, Donna's water broke, and we raced back down to the hospital yet again.

On January 23rd, Donna gave birth to Nicole via C-section. Apparently, Netta was also born extremely premature, and since Donna had a C-section when she was born, it was required that the same procedure be administered for Nicole's arrival. Initially, I had my reservations about witnessing the procedure, due to being rather squeamish, but I quickly got over those feelings once I saw her emerging from Donna's body. I was overwhelmed with both joy and anxiety.

She was so tiny, weighing two pounds and eleven ounces. She was also routinely placed in an incubator in the hospital's Neonatal Intensive Care Unit until she reached a safe weight and was able to consume food on her own. Unfortunately, our bundle of joy was unable to come home for two whole months. Three days after

Nicole was born, Donna was released to go home. The plan she and I came up with was to get Netta back into her regular daily routine so she wouldn't drive herself crazy worrying about her sister. So once Donna returned home, we all would travel extensively for the next 60 days.

Between chauffeuring Netta to and from school, returning to work, and going back and forth to the hospital to see Nicole, I was mentally, spiritually, and physically exhausted. I continued to recite the old scripture that states, "To whom much is given, much is required." That quote, along with prayer, constantly provided me with the strength needed to keep pushing on and serving as the rock my family needed.

Surprises (2013)

Toward the end of March, we received word that Nicole would finally be free to come home. The past few months were so taxing for Donna and me that it was tough to see an end in sight. We were able to remain hopeful through the power of prayer. Throughout the entire ordeal, we received unwavering support from a few surprising sources once everyone found out our newborn was going to be in the hospital for an extended period of time. The two sources were my coworkers and many of the students from my 4th-period Advanced Language Arts class.

One afternoon when school ended, I was called to the media center. Unbeknownst to me, my colleagues had put together a surprise baby shower for Donna, which she was unable to attend since she was at the hospital with Nicole. I was so overwhelmed by the gesture that I shed a few inconspicuous tears. There were so many diapers, wipes, and other items that I could barely fit them all in my car. The other event occurred the following week. A bunch of my students got together and created a huge, makeshift postcard for my wife and daughter. They also handed me an envelope with about 100 dollars. Apparently, they collected the money from their peers in my class, without me knowing. The thoughtful and selfless gesture blew me away. I couldn't believe what they did for my family. It was one of the most memorable moments in my teaching career.

The day we were set to bring Nicole home was surreal. The night before, I could barely sleep, so I spent time making sure everything was prepared for her arrival. Since we only had a two-bedroom apartment at the time, her crib would have to be stationed in our room. After putting it together, I double-checked the crib to ensure it was sturdy and safe for her. While driving down to the hospital, I replayed in my mind what it would feel like to hold our precious miracle baby in my arms, finally. The more I attempted to envision how things would play out, the faster I drove.

When Donna, Netta, and I arrived at the hospital, we were anxious as we got on the elevator. As Nicole was discharged and we got in the car, I drove as slowly as possible, not wanting her to awaken from her peaceful slumber. On our way from the hospital, we took a couple of detours before we made it home. The first place we stopped was Granny's apartment, so she and my dad could see the baby. Conveniently, Granny lived less than 5 minutes away from the hospital. Granny was so happy to see all of us, especially the baby. My dad seemed so distant mentally, though he was physically there. He smiled a lot when we were at the apartment, but he didn't really say too much, which was odd. Usually, my dad was ultra-lively, funny, and talkative. I could look in his eyes and tell that something was wrong. I didn't push the issue, though, because it was the first day of our newborn's release. Granny pulled me to the side and told me I needed to make sure I spend time with my dad more often. Something serious was going on with him that I wasn't aware of. I told myself I'll try to reach out to him at least 2 to 3 times a week.

After we left Granny's, we drove east to Hollywood to take Nicole to see my uncle and Lapolean, who was a football coach at Flanagan High School at the time. We would spend 30 minutes to an hour at my uncle's house, and then we'd finally hop on I-95 to take the 45-minute drive back home. We were able to pull up to our apartment before it got dark outside. I believe we all were relieved to make it home, especially Nicole. Netta was in the backseat with her, making kissy faces and talking to her the entire time. The first thing we did was lie down on the couch as a family and breathe a sigh of relief. At last, our family felt complete.

Family Fallout (2013)

I always took pride in my loyalty, especially when it pertained to the people I loved. A rather unfortunate situation transpired when I was unintentionally pocket-dialed on a Saturday afternoon. I overheard one of my family members speaking with my uncle in the car; they were engaged in a conversation that consisted of a few critical comments about my wife and me.

Earlier that day, I had previously spoken to that family member, and they stated I needed to come down south to spend more time with my dad (Part of me knew I needed to do a better job of that). I told them I'd try to visit Broward County when I could, because we were dealing with a few serious situations impacting our household. The issues consisted of my wife's surprising health diagnosis (massive fibroids that were giving her constant stomach pain), the daily demands of work, as well as the continuous fatherly responsibilities I had to take care of, especially since Donna wasn't doing well. Through prayer and my faith in God, I was staying afloat, even though it was still mentally and physically taxing. Growing up, I wish someone had explained to me how difficult it was to maintain my roles as a husband, father, and provider.

Nevertheless, while eavesdropping during the candid conversation those particular members of my family were having, I heard them say fibroids weren't a big deal because they also had them at one point in time, and they were successfully surgically removed. Little did they know, Donna's doctor advised her that there could be some complications that could occur during the recommended fibroid surgery. He mentioned once she's cut open,

263

she could be exposed to all sorts of things, which could potentially lead to, in the worst-case scenario, death, and that was definitely not something I'd take lightly. So, when I heard the concerning comments from my relative's phone conversation, I was fire hot.

After a few more choice words about me and my decisions, as well as Donna's health condition, I heard my uncle verbally cosign the sentiments, and I lost it. I immediately hung up the phone and called them back, and said, "You may not know this, but you all pocket dialed me by mistake, and I heard everything you all said during your conversation. I can't believe you all feel that way! Y'all are minimizing a serious situation that involves my wife and her health. It's all good; I see how y'all are. Don't worry about it. I got a trick for that!"

Afterward, I hung up the phone. With the amount of rage I felt, I knew it was best for me to keep my distance from them for a little while to avoid further confrontations. Needless to say, "a little while" would become years. I let my emotions get the best of me, even though I knew deep down, I could've handled things better than I did.

The Season (Jan-Mar 2013)

Between the time Nicole was born and when she was in the hospital for months, I still helped out with the basketball team whenever I could, though I wasn't as dedicated as I was before I got married. My priorities were different, and I had to find a way to slowly but surely pull away from coaching. I remembered a member of our faculty approaching me about possibly taking over the head coaching position once Coach Mitch retired. I told him I doubted I could dedicate the time needed to keep the JFK legacy alive.

During the current season, we had players who were good athletes. The problem with this particular team was that they didn't have the typical athlete mindset. Their focus was primarily on looking the part and perfecting the tough-guy image. In our previous years together, Coach Mitch and I had a history of getting through to players known to be rough around the edges. This year was different. We had constant issues with their behavior in school as well as on the court. It was a train wreck from the start.

With everything that was transpiring with my family, I couldn't focus on helping our players get themselves together like I used to. The season came and went like a wild tornado. We had a decent regular season while getting blown out of the gym in the playoffs against our rivals, Roosevelt Middle. Regardless of the reason why, the loss was still disappointing. Coach Mitch told me next year's season will be better because most of our "attitude problems" on the team will be heading off to high school by then, and we'll be able to start over with a clean slate.

Abrupt End to Coaching (2014)

When the new school year started, rumblings and rumors were going around campus about our school's administration taking a different direction regarding the boys' basketball team. I told Coach Mitch about the rumors I heard through the grapevine, and he immediately went to our athletic director to inquire about the rumors. Lo and behold, Coach Mitch was told the principal wanted to open up all coaching positions, which would mean Mitch would have to interview for the position he had held for 20+ years. We knew what that meant; they had already decided to move on and basically hire someone else for the coaching position. So, when the time came for interviews,

Mitch went through the motions of interviewing, and sure enough, they chose someone else. The crazy thing about it was that someone close to the administration asked me if I was interested in continuing as an assistant coach for the new coach who was hired. I respectfully declined. Besides, now that Donna had returned to work, I would have to help pick Netta up from aftercare by no later than 4:00 a few days each week. With my job being 25 to 28 minutes away and my school ending at 3:30 P.M., I would have to leave work as soon as the last bell rang to ensure I would make it to pick her up in time.

As far as Nicole was concerned, she would spend a day (sometimes two) during the weekday at her godparent's house while we were all at work. Since they didn't live too far from Donna's job in Pembroke Pines, she would drop Nicole off with them early in the morning and pick her up at night. The Stanleys were definitely lifesavers because we could not imagine trusting

266

anyone else to watch over her at that time, especially going through all the complications she's gone through. For about a year, Donna's strategic schedule consisted of working three 12-hour shifts, one to two days during the weekend, and one to two days during the weekday. Since I was no longer coaching basketball, I had a lot of time on my hands.

Donna and I decided to dedicate our free time to looking into finding a house to move into. We knew Nicole would eventually need her own room, and there was no use in waiting until the last minute to make a move. We spent about a month looking for our first house. The entire process was tedious and exhausting. Some houses were downright terrible. We couldn't believe our realtor took us to some of the properties. At the time, we had already been through two realtors: one named Jean, who was recommended to us by one of Donna's cousins.

The other one, whose name was Jodi, was found online by Donna. Jean took us to a few homes that were not up to par, in our opinion. The majority of them were either too small or in less-than-desirable locations. The other realtor, Jodi, wasn't much better. The properties she took Donna and me to were horrendous. Two of the homes stuck out more than the others. One was structured like a two-story cabin right beside a drug rehabilitation facility, and the other was a two-story home with a massive hole in the roof.

All seemed lost until we tried our hand one final time with another realtor, a friend of the family, recommended. At that time, our perseverance paid off! We finally found a house we were intrigued by in a community named "Strawberry Lakes," which was located in the western portion of Lake Worth. It was a nice 3-bedroom, 2-bathroom home with an additional kitchen on the back patio. In the backyard, there were many fruit trees, such as mango, banana, soursop, and avocado. We saw a lot of potential in that particular house as a cool starter home for us, so we put in an offer, and it was accepted after a few days of back-and-forth between our realtor and the seller's realtor. We were overjoyed and completely caught off guard by the many blessings God bestowed upon us so quickly since Donna and I got married.

Not too long after our offer was accepted, we officially moved in November, right in time for Thanksgiving. Grace and one of my coworkers, who I went to college with, volunteered to help us move, which was nice. When we were all moved in, I took a moment to go into the backyard and pray, thanking God for our new home. It was certainly the type of achievement I couldn't have imagined occurring years ago. Shortly after getting everything situated, we had an exciting housewarming event within a few weeks to celebrate with a few friends, coworkers, my dad, my sister, and Donna's mother.

My Dad Goes Missing (2014)

One evening after coming home from work, I received a phone call from Granny stating my dad had gone missing. I was also told that it wasn't the first time it occurred, which surprised me. She also said my uncle found him walking down 32nd Avenue in the Opa Locka area. After speaking with her, I figured he was walking around or near some of the places he and I used to frequent when we were living on the street back in the day.

Donna and I drove down to Miami to search for my dad, and the first place we went was around the corner from the house he grew up in. Considering his mental health was on rapid decline, we were worried something tragic would happen if we didn't quickly find him. Lo and behold, we spotted him walking down 32nd Avenue in Opa Locka. When we pulled up beside him as he was walking southbound, I called out to him from the driver's side window. When he heard my voice, he looked, grinned, and walked toward the car and got into the backseat.

On our way toward Granny's apartment to return my dad, there was an eerie silence the entire time. I started to ask him about his outrageously long walk, but I decided not to, and I chalked the whole ordeal up to his declining mental state. The main thing I realized was that my dad was never going to be the same again.

Unexpected Request (Dec 2013)

One evening, while Netta and I were watching television, she looked over at me and asked if I was sad since I wasn't coaching at my school anymore. I stared at her for a second or two in amazement. I couldn't believe she asked me that question out of the blue like that. Furthermore, I asked her what made her ask, and she said she knew how much I loved coaching basketball. Moreover, I told her, "Yes, I love basketball, but I love my family more." She looked at me with confusion, as if she didn't understand what I meant, and I explained that my responsibilities as a husband and a father come before coaching. The bottom line was, I didn't have the time to coach anymore.

Considering Netta was only seven years old, I didn't expect her to fully understand what I meant. She then hit me with a question that came completely out of left field. She asked me why I didn't teach her how to play. My eyes lit up, and an imaginary lightbulb went off in my head. With a sheepish grin on my face, I asked her if she really wanted to learn, and she said, "Yes!" I didn't push the issue, and I just responded with a simple "Okay." In my head, though, the wheels were definitely turning. I'd already formulated a plan to start showing her the fundamentals of the game to see if she'd enjoy learning how to play.

My first objective was to purchase a basketball hoop, and I knew Walmart was the best place to get one, since it was just about time for Christmas. They were known for having awesome holiday deals, and there was one located extremely close to our house. Furthermore, within 24 hours of the conversation Netta and I had, I brought a hoop home. Within the next few days, after putting the goal together and setting it up in our lengthy eight-car driveway, Netta and I went to work.

The first thing I showed her was how to do a proper layup. Considering she was left-handed, and I was right-handed, I had to be mindful of that when teaching and demonstrating everything. Netta caught on rather quickly, and I knew from that point forward she was more than capable of developing nicely. During the first full week of instruction, I'd teach her certain basic skills, such as dribbling, proper footwork, and the differences between how and when to perform left-hand versus right-hand layups. She was very eager to learn, and I knew that was a recipe for greatness.

From December 2013 to the beginning of September 2014, I trained Netta almost every day straight. To avoid burnout and redundancy, the key strategy I used was ensuring every day was fun. Using random YouTube videos, along with my previous coaching and streetball experience, I was able to formulate a weekly schedule that offered a variety of activities I knew she'd enjoy, all while improving one day at a time. We would occasionally watch women's college basketball games, primarily the March Madness Tournament games, so she could see how some of the best of the best play the game at a high level.

From May to August, Netta and I would watch live WNBA basketball games on television in the evenings, and she would become an avid fan of basketball legend Maya Moore. Through her awesome abilities and unwavering faith, she would become the motivation Netta needed to strive to play competitively. She'd ask me if I thought she could play like the people on television played, and my response was, "Of course, as long as you work for it, you'll be able to accomplish anything you set your mind on." I always stressed to her that regardless of what she wanted to do in life, she

271

would have to keep God first, and things would work out the way they were intended to.

***

Little did Netta know, I had already signed her up for the 7-9-year-old co-ed youth league in Boynton Beach, which ran from the second week of September to the latter part of November. When I told Donna about it, I could tell she was a bit apprehensive at first; after a while, she warmed up to the idea after realizing how much hard work Netta put into getting better every day. Netta, on the other hand, was nervous when she found out, though I advised her that she was going to "try it out" to see how it went. Once the league started, Netta was clearly one of the best players there. She was fundamentally sound, and she could also do things on the court that the majority of the boys in the league couldn't, such as dribbling without double dribbling and making layups with both hands consistently. Parents, the referees, and spectators were in awe of how polished she looked during games.

Now that Netta had actual games to look forward to throughout the week, whenever we spent time in our driveway working out, we would focus on game-time situations. I would teach her not only how to play the game, but also how to think about the game. For instance, if a defender attempted to steal the ball away from her, she could counter and use certain moves to get away or get by them. When it was time to play in the games, she would practically use the moves she was taught to dominate her opponents. Her first experience playing basketball was a huge success because it helped her acquire confidence. Donna and I realized Netta was a beast on the court, but the problem was that there weren't many girls in the area who played basketball, as far as we knew.

After Netta's first recreation season at the JCC, I knew I had to keep her going because I didn't want practicing in the driveway or at the local park to become too repetitive. When one league ended, I would always do my due diligence to find another for her to play in. I would end up taking her to play in leagues and camps from as far as Wellington down to Boynton Beach. When she played in her first all-girl league in Wellington, she dominated from the beginning, even though she was one of the youngest players there. Ironically, in every league we put her in, she was always two years younger than most of the girls and/or young men she played with.

That move was strategic because I knew that once she eventually got into middle and high school, playing against kids her age would be a walk in the park. At every recreation league she played in, she'd earn a trophy, medal, or some recognition, and one would think she would start to acquire a certain level of ego or cockiness, not Netta. She knew she was good, but she never realized just how good she really was, regardless of what people said to her or the awards she earned. She had a natural humbleness that couldn't be taught or manufactured.

Well-Rounded (2016)

Aside from basketball, there were other things Netta was interested in, and I made sure she was exposed to them. For instance, I knew she loved animals from watching many wildlife-focused shows, such as "Call of the Wildman," "Gator Boyz," and others.

Occasionally, I would set up opportunities for her to attend various events throughout Broward and Palm Beach to be around many of the animals she'd seen on television. She said she enjoyed each opportunity, and it made me happy because I was able to do for her what wasn't done for me growing up. In no way did I view myself as the perfect father figure, though I tried to be.

In addition to animals, I also made sure she understood her source of strength didn't come from anything physical but from the Holy Spirit. I constantly taught Netta about the importance of prayer and living a Christ-filled life to the best of her abilities. We would have many conversations about life in general, and she would ask me many intriguing questions about some of the questionable things she'd hear about or see on television.

One day, while working out, she asked me something that totally caught me off guard; she asked, "Why does it seem like most girls who play basketball try to act like they're men?" When I asked her what she meant, she said some of the players in the WNBA she watches on TV get their hair cut like men, and some even get a bunch of tattoos. Then, she proceeded to say that many of the girls she knows who play basketball also date other girls. I asked her how she felt about it, and she said she finds it gross. She also added, "And it's a sin!" I breathed a sigh of relief because, as a parent, sometimes you don't know what to expect to come out of a young, impressionable child's mouth. Thank God we were doing our jobs as parents with Christian values. I also advised her not to avoid or mistreat people based on their choice of lifestyle; instead, she should serve as a living and breathing example of someone who lives for Christ.

She was adamant about setting an example for girls around the world by promoting the message that they don't have to compromise who they are to fit in with what everyone else was doing. After our heart-to-heart conversation and a quick prayer, I could tell in my spirit her journey was bigger than basketball. It was apparent that Netta had a special calling on her life, and I was determined to help her flourish in any way possible.

Travel Ball Experiment (2016)

At the conclusion of the all-girls rec league in Wellington, we were approached by a parent from the area who wanted to put a fifth-grade girls travel team together under the Wellington Wolves brand. Since Netta was only in the third grade, we were a bit hesitant, but the parent insisted we give it a try. He stated that Netta would be great for the team, regardless of her age. He also acknowledged that she can hoop with the best of them.

We decided to let her play, even though she didn't really care one way or the other; she just wanted to play with other girls she knew consistently. I guess bouncing from league to league and gym to gym really started to take its toll on her. That decision ended up being one of the worst decisions we made at the time because Netta went from dominating in the rec league to barely touching the court during the short but embarrassing travel season. Though most of the girls on Netta's team were in the fifth grade, their team would end up playing against sixth-grade teams in local tournaments due to not having many fifth-grade teams in the area.

We would travel around the Palm Beach and Broward County areas to play against bigger, faster, and more experienced teams just to get blown out by 50 to 60 points every game. They would only play in a handful of tournaments, but between the confidence-shaking losses and barely touching the court, Netta finally broke down after the last tournament and cried because she didn't know why she was seemingly punished with not receiving the same playing time as the other girls. That day, I made a promise to her that she would never go through a situation like that ever again, as long as I could help it.

After that debacle of a travel season, I would take Netta out to the local outside basketball courts at John Prince Park to play pickup games with high school boys and grown men. Struggling against the fellas showed her she would have to continue to work on her game behind the scenes to get to the level she said she wanted to make it to.

At that time, Donna was working hard behind the scenes, working to earn her master's degree. I picked up the slack again as far as the cooking, cleaning, and taking care of the girls was concerned. I really didn't want her to worry about anything but going to work and getting her assignments done. Many nights I stayed up with her to keep her company, and then I'd proofread her essays before she submitted them.

As for my schedule, it was terribly hectic, but I knew it would all be worth it in the end. It was a little tough keeping our youngest daughter, Nicole, occupied while her mom was on her educational grind. After a while, she started coming outside when Netta and I were in our driveway working out. She would join in some of the drills, and it was obvious she had been watching us work out together for some time. She even went as far as telling me she wanted to play basketball too.

When I signed Netta up to play in the next co-ed rec league in Lake Worth, I signed her sister up to play as well. Netta's team played after Nicole's team every Saturday morning. At the conclusion of the league, a local coaching legend by the name of Melissa offered to put a travel team together consisting of Netta and other girls from the community, who were also pretty good.

Donna and I felt more comfortable with Coach Melissa than Netta's previous travel coach at Wellington, so we decided to give her a shot. From day one of practice, we could tell she knew how much talent Netta had, and she wouldn't let it go to waste. She took her time to teach the girls not only about basketball but life as a whole, which we appreciated. The vision she had quickly came to fruition, and the team proved to be very good, with Netta as the starting point guard and leading scorer. It was a tremendous experience, and at the conclusion of the travel season, they surprisingly made it to the AAU championship game against the Lady Titans from Melbourne. Even though Netta's team lost in a blowout, she still earned an Outstanding Player of the Tournament plaque, and during the game, she hit her first-ever three-point shot in a game. Before that, she was always afraid to shoot from that far during live action because she didn't want to potentially shoot an airball and embarrass herself.

The following year was more of the same, with the key difference that Coach Melissa asked me to take over the head coaching duties while she shifted to an assistant position. It was a decent season for the team. Once again, we lost in the AAU championship game in Fort Pierce to the Tampa Aces, which was a team coached by WNBA legend Candace Parker's brother. Again, just like last travel ball season, Netta played a wonderful game. Still, her teammates severely underperformed, and the second-best player on the team didn't play due to a recurring injury to her kneecap. Netta played well enough to earn another Outstanding Player of the Tournament plaque. After the season, Coach Melissa told me it was time for Netta to "hit the circuit" and gain national exposure because of her abilities. Coach stated Netta wouldn't get that exposure continuing to play against local teams within Florida. It was truly a difficult conversation to have as a parent, but I understood Coach's point; she felt it was time to "Leave the Nest." At that point, I would have to find a travel team that could provide her with what she needed and deserved: a chance to compete against other top-tier players.

Sacrifices (2017)

Before the end of the 2016-2017 school year, I decided to make the difficult decision not to return to JFK the following year. Don't get me wrong, I loved the kids and my colleagues there, but since Netta would be heading to middle school the following year, there was no way I would allow her to go to school there. She was beyond sheltered, and I'd seen some of the best and brightest become products of their environment throughout my time there. Between the constant fights, heavy influence of gang culture, drug use, and weapons that were found on or near campus, it was just too much for Netta to be able to handle.

I planned to look for a new school to teach at while I was on summer vacation. The trickiest part was informing my principal that I wouldn't be returning. I knew it would be a troublesome thing to do since I was constantly told how valuable I was not only to the school but also to the entire community in Riviera Beach. Donna advised me to tell him the truth and let the chips fall where they may. That's what I decided to do. He told me he understood exactly where I was coming from. He said he respected my decision, not only as a man but also as a father.

Of course, when I informed my students and colleagues I wouldn't be returning, they were upset. When they were told why I was leaving, some of my students urged me to bring my daughter to JFK, while others applauded me for not even considering it. When the current school year concluded, I applied for a vacant language arts position at Polo Park, an A-rated middle school in the Wellington area. The peculiar thing about it was that I never heard back from them. During Netta's most recent travel season, I heard quite a few of her teammates were 7th graders from Palm Springs Middle School. Though I had never heard of the school before, I was curious to know its intricate details. I asked the kids and their parents, and everyone had nothing but great things to say about it.

I decided to apply for a vacant teaching position that the school had posted on the district's website. I heard back within a few weeks with an interview date and time. During the interview, I spoke about my background, teaching experience, and my immediate family. The principal reminded me that, per district policy, I would be able to bring my daughter to any school where I worked, which I already knew. After the success of the interview, I was offered a job on the spot, which I graciously accepted. The cherry on top was finding out the school had a pretty good girl's basketball team she could be a part of as well.

Dad's Health (2017)

After a while, my dad was finally approved to receive his full benefits from Veteran Affairs. He had been given a room at the local VA assisted living facility in Pembroke Pines.

My sister would provide me with weekly updates, and she informed me that he was diagnosed with Dementia, Alzheimer's, and Parkinson's disease. He was no longer able to talk and walk on his own, and I couldn't bring myself to see him like that.

From time to time, I would make my way down to the facility to sit with him for a few hours or so. I would always make sure I'd visit when the coast was clear. The last thing I wanted to do was visit when any of my other family members were there; I wasn't in the mood for a potential back-and-forth that could lead to any issues where my dad was being taken care of. I'd go up there with Grace off and on, but most of the time I was by myself.

When sitting with him, all I could think about was the good old days, before we moved to Miami, when he was still in the Army.

A New Environment (2017-2018)

The first year at the new job site was an adventure, especially with Netta going to school with me every day. Since she was an introvert, I knew it would take a little time for her to adjust. At the very beginning of the year, it was apparent that my classroom was her safe haven early in the mornings before school began, until she got her bearings and started to acquire friends and associates.

Before I knew it, many of the toughest and most outgoing students from the 8th grade gravitated towards her. Once they found out she was a talented basketball player, they treated her like she was an upperclassman, instead of a typical 6th grader. Pretty soon, she stopped hanging out in my room before school started and began chilling with her peers in the cafeteria as well as the courtyard. Although she was always a bit of an introvert, she became popular quickly. We both had rather favorable reputations throughout the campus; I was labeled as the cool, down-to-earth teacher who always dressed professionally, and Netta was loved by all of her teachers and peers due to her laid-back demeanor.

Thankfully, both of our transitions to Palm Springs were great. At the beginning of the year, right before basketball season started, I was asked to be one of the assistant coaches. When the current head coach heard about my past coaching experience, he figured I would be an asset to the team. The season went well. We were undefeated throughout the regular season, and Netta asserted her dominance from tryouts to the playoff game we eventually lost to Boca Raton Middle in overtime. The worst thing about the loss was that Netta was carrying the team on her back the entire game, until she fouled out in the 4th quarter. All in all, her dominant season led to her earning quite a reputation throughout the county. It was time to find an upper-echelon travel team on which she could display her talents.

The biggest issue with Netta's success on the basketball court was the amount of time spent ensuring she would be the best version of herself. I always told her that if she ever got to a point where she wanted to stop playing, she could (as long as she found another activity to be involved in). I even tried to persuade her to take up other sports like track and field or volleyball, but she wasn't interested. The amount of focus placed on Netta drove an insurmountable wedge between my wife and me. Donna told me she felt I was overly fixated on Netta's development instead of maintaining some semblance of balance.

After she repeatedly relayed that message to me, I realized over time that she was right, and I became more cognizant of what I dedicated my time to. At that point, I knew I needed to put more effort into our marriage. Once a week for the next few weeks, I'd ensure the two of us went out on date nights to grab a bite to eat and enjoy each other's presence.

Searching for A Team (2018)

I searched high and low for a travel team in the Palm Beach area that could help Netta get the exposure she deserved. The only organization I found was the Palm Beach Starzz in Palm Beach Gardens. Once I reached out to the director of the organization, we set up some time for Netta to work out with a few of their players. The 3-point shooting drills Coach Pat had them doing were impressive.

From the start, I could see how beneficial the drills he had them doing were. I liked the intensity the coach showed when dealing with the players. After the workout, Netta said she was a bit intimidated, but she felt she would get better there. Unfortunately, the organization folded after playing in a local tournament due to low numbers.

As a result, Coach Pat asked us to attend a showcase event with Elite Coastal United in Northern Florida. Ironically, ECU was actually the same organization Netta played against in the AAU championship game a few years ago. The showcase was not what we expected. There was local media coverage and a slew of talent there from all over. My nerves were bad because I didn't know if the environment was too much for her. The last thing I'd want to do is set her up for disappointment.

Thankfully, Netta put on a show and earned an MVP award during the event. She was even asked to join their 8th-grade Elite Travel Team, which would help her receive national exposure. There were a few catches to the invitation we were informed of after the fact. The practices were on the weekend in North Florida, and they also wanted her to play on their 6th-grade team as well as the 8th-grade Elite Team. The director of their organization pitched that Netta would lead the 6th-grade team and also play on the elite team with the eighth graders.

When the tournaments started, it was clear that Netta was the best player on the 6th-grade team. The 8th-grade team was a different story, though. The team was centered around a 7th-grade phenom named Emily. Netta played well with the older team, even though her playing time was limited. The upsetting part was that we were led to believe she would have the chance to be a solid contributor on the elite team, rather than being given spoon-fed minutes and playing the meaningless 6th-grade games from start to finish. It felt as if they were using her. She averaged twenty points per game with the 6th-grade team and 6 points per game with the other team (in about five to six minutes of playing time). That nearly broke her spirits yet again. All I could think of was the Wellington Wolves experience from a few years back, all over again. I felt as if I lied to her by telling her she wouldn't go through that situation ever again. Therefore, after the last tournament of the season, I had an uncomfortable conversation with the head coach, informing him that we would not be bringing Netta back next travel season.

New Experiences (2018-2019)

The following year, I made a New Year's resolution to try to balance my focus more evenly between spending more time with my wife, Nicole, and Netta. The catch to that goal was that Netta's middle school basketball coach decided to shake things up and focus more on his family and a business he was starting outside of school. He essentially left the head coaching position to me. I was both thrilled and nervous, because I didn't want to lose focus on my vow to focus more on my marriage than basketball.

I had a heart-to-heart with my wife, and she gave me her blessing to coach as long as I put effort into making sure we would continue our date nights. Donna and Netta were happy about the coaching change because they felt I might have the opportunity to lead the team to a district championship, something the school had never experienced before.

During the early portion of the school year, I'd teach Nicole how to ride a bike without training wheels. I also started experimenting with allowing Netta to drive my car around our neighborhood while I was in the passenger seat, of course. She was so scared of the idea of "racking out" that she refused to drive more than 10 miles per hour. The current school year would be like any other year, smoother than the other side of the pillow. The majority of my students loved and appreciated being in my class because of my unorthodox teaching strategies and failed attempts at humor. Regardless, all of them knew I cared about their well-being, and they looked forward to learning from me every day. I also enjoyed having real-world conversations with them that would cause them to think critically. Nearly all of my colleagues were impressed with the rapport I had with all the students I came in contact with. When it was time for basketball season, I was eager to run the team a little differently than before. I placed a significant emphasis on hard-nosed man-to-man defense. I told the team they would need to defend at a high level to prepare them not only to contend for a championship but also to get ready for high school. Offensively, we all knew where the bulk of our points would come from, between Netta and her teammates E.Z. and Gray. Defensively, though, I would need to develop a theme for the season to keep the girls engaged and motivated.

After careful deliberation, I came up with an idea of focusing on limiting our opponents to less than 15 points per game. I told the girls that if they allowed a team to score 15 or more points, they would have to run the stairs at the school the next day in practice. All in all, the regular season was great. We only allowed one team to score more than 10 points (L.C. Swain scored 21), and we scored over 450 points in ten regular-season games. Our opponents scored only 65 points against us that year. Since E.Z. was an 8th grader and Netta was a 7th grader, I decided to take Netta off the point guard spot and let E.Z. run the show and play point. The goal was to help her acquire the confidence she needed for high school next year. The setup worked like a charm. "E" was super aggressive all regular season, and she was able to lead the way offensively. Most of the time, the starters didn't play much during the second half of most of our games due to the massive blowouts and running clocks.

The bad thing was the season ended with another playoff loss to Don Estridge, 37-33. They had an awesome tandem in the post, and we really didn't have an answer for it. Netta earned another MVP award, though the sting of another playoff disappointment would hurt just as much as realizing that maybe we both could've done more to finally get over the hump and secure a middle school playoff win. I felt as if I let Netta and her teammates down by not making the necessary adjustments during critical points in the game. I told myself, "There's always next year."

During the latter part of the middle school season, Netta and I drove down to Somerset Academy in Broward to have her try out for the "Team Knight" travel team. Team Knight was a team named after former NBA basketball player Brandon Knight. From the first day of tryouts, everyone affiliated with the program could see Netta's talent level as she competed against young ladies who were two and three years older than her. She made the organization's fourteen-and-under team, which was filled with some of the best talent from as far away as Fort Myers to Miami, Florida. They'd travel the country, playing against many of the top fifteen-and-under teams. They were highly competitive in the majority of the tournaments they played in. Netta got along well with her teammates and went on to earn a few accolades throughout March and April for her stellar performances. There were a few statewide girls' basketball publication companies that took note of her and her teammate's exceptional play.

At the conclusion of the basketball season, we were contacted by the head girls' varsity basketball coach at Heritage, a big-time private school in Palm Beach. He wanted to recruit Netta to attend his school to play ball, and he made an interesting pitch that we strongly considered. He told us he was building a competitive program, and Netta would be a major addition to his team. Not only that, but he also recommended that I apply to teach at the school to make the process easier, if I wanted. The rule of thumb at their school was that if someone worked there, their kids would have a better chance of getting in without a problem. I took a wild stab in the dark and applied for a middle school English/Language Arts position.

Unbeknownst to me, I received a call from someone from their administrative team for an interview. During this time, Donna had Netta go through the process of taking their standard tests and applying in advance, just in case. After an excellent interview, I was asked to set up a time to come in and teach a mock lesson to a random ELA class. The great thing about it was that I could decide what mini-lesson to teach and how to teach it. Needless to say, I killed the mini-lesson so effectively that the students in the class asked me if I could come back and be their new teacher. I was flattered.

After a few days, I received another phone call from an administrator at Heritage. They offered me a job, but the catch was that they wanted me to teach a "special group of students" who were facing some unique challenges. I was also told that those particular students were housed in a strategic location on campus. As an educator for as long as I have been one, I knew that meant students with emotional/behavioral disabilities. She also mentioned I'd "be able to connect with the students easily based on my background." That phrase was an indirect way of informing me that the students were also black. I wasn't too thrilled about the offer due to how it was presented. I felt there were other underlying reasons why they wanted to hire me, and it didn't have anything to do with my intellect or my professional background.

I decided not to take the job, but the possibility of letting Netta go to school there was still up in the air until we found out what we would have to pay and/or contribute to the school. After the application was completed and Netta had taken and passed all the required tests, we were told we would have to pay a particular amount of money for her to attend their school. We were given the option to either pay or work on campus to cover the fees.

Once they found out my wife was a nurse, we were told she could work in the nurse's office (for free) to work off the hours/money throughout the day, or we could clean up the campus after hours. We were beyond livid. I told them we weren't committing to doing either one since we were approached about our daughter potentially coming to their school to play basketball. We felt disrespected until we found out there are many families on campus performing duties to supplement their fees, but we weren't going for it. Needless to say, we respectfully declined Netta's invitation to attend their school.

Humbling Experience (Apr 2019)

At the end of March, during Spring Break, I took Netta to John Prince to play some pickup basketball against the fellas who normally frequented the park. During one of the games we were playing, a player from the opposing team had to leave, and one of the spectators decided to take his place. The issue with this particular 6'4, 310-pound guy was that he wore slides instead of basketball shoes. Normally, I wouldn't play with someone who didn't have shoes on, but we were only a few points away from winning the game. Little did I know it would be a costly mistake.

Amongst the constant battle down low in the post between the two of us, buddy stumbled and fell on my left foot with all of his weight. After the dude fell, he got back up as if nothing had happened, but when I fell, there was an instantaneous pop, and I immediately clutched my leg in agony. Not realizing how serious the injury was, Netta walked over to me and said, "You alright? Aye, it's game point, you're tough, right? Come on, so we can finish this game." I was beyond surprised by her reaction, and I quickly told her I couldn't put any weight on my foot while she was helping me off the ground. We ended up losing the game since I couldn't move. The big guy I was trying to guard scored the game-winning bucket, while I just stood there, defenseless.

After the game, Netta held my basketball and car keys while I slowly and surely hopped to the car on one leg, like a crazy person. After finally making it to my vehicle, my foot was obviously completely swollen. As I cranked the car, I knew it would be a tall task attempting to drive home. I contemplated letting Netta drive us to the house, but I didn't want to risk the police pulling us over and getting a laundry list of unnecessary charges. While driving, I told Netta to call her mom and tell her what happened. The pain and throbbing I was experiencing at the time were unbearable. It got to the point where I started giggling hysterically for some strange reason. Once we made it to our driveway, Netta had to help me get out and into the house through our garage. It was a tedious task that required patience due to the seriousness of the situation.

After getting to the couch in the living room, Donna had to cut my shoe off with the hospital-grade scissors she had in her work bag. While she was cutting, I'd chuckle hysterically, which was both weird and fascinating. Netta asked Donna why I was laughing so much, and she said I was in shock. My foot was so swollen that she had to rush me to the emergency room after wrapping my foot with an ace bandage. After getting there, it seemed as if the pain had subsided a bit until one of the nurses went to unwrap the ace bandage. I yelled so loud, you would've thought someone was trying to kill me. We found out I would have to go to a specialist to have my broken foot repaired.

The surgery wouldn't take too long, but I had a feeling the biggest issue would be the recovery time. The doctor required me to keep my foot elevated at all times while I was healing. As crazy as it may seem, I really hated the idea of missing weeks of work because I knew my students wouldn't receive quality instruction from a substitute teacher. I wasn't concerned about any financial ramifications because I had over 600 hours of sick time saved up from my twelve years in education.

The rather unfortunate part of my recovery process was the fact that my immediate family didn't take into consideration the mental anguish someone like me would experience. I couldn't just get up and go whenever I wanted, and that weighed heavily on me mentally. I took pride in the fact that I was known as "Mr. Reliable." I was so used to being the person everyone could depend on when things needed to be done that it was torture for me not to be able to take care of anyone or anything, including myself. Around that time, I started to experience occasional bouts of depression.

The ordeal would lead to constant arguments and back-and-forths between Donna and me. Maybe it wasn't fair to project my feelings onto her, but I just felt she was supposed to have an open mind and understand what I was experiencing as a health care professional. After a while, it seemed as if she resented the fact that I was laid up and unable to do the things I'd typically do. I knew it was a lot for her to carry the load of the entire household while I was incapacitated, but there wasn't anything I could do. Maybe I was just in my own head, but just maybe I wasn't. One thing was for sure: it was pretty easy to see the shift in attitude as time went by.

Near Fatal Accident (2019)

While in the midst of recovering from my surgery, Donna and I spoke sparingly, and mainly on an as-needed basis. She was giving me the typical silent treatment when she was upset with me about something. Unexpectedly, tragedy potentially struck when Donna was involved in a terrible automobile accident. She was driving in West Palm and was struck by a car in a head-on collision. The police were chasing the young lady in the other car because she was the getaway driver for someone who was committing a home burglary at the time. She ran through a red light and hit Donna as she was entering an intersection.

As I was lying in bed, with my foot elevated, my cellphone rang, and it was a number I didn't recognize. Usually, I wouldn't answer calls from unknown numbers, but something told me to answer the phone during that time. It was a case worker from the Good Samaritan Hospital calling to tell me my wife was involved in a car accident. She also advised me she was going to be ok; they were going to run tests to ensure there were no serious injuries she sustained. I quickly hung up the phone, with every intention of making my way to the hospital.

First, I had to make plans for Netta and her sister to get home from school. I called Nicole's school and let them know what was going on. Then I called Donna's mom, and she offered to come up to Palm Beach to pick up Netta and her sister from their schools. While making travel arrangements for the girls, I tried to ensure I didn't accidentally bang my foot on the car's interior while maneuvering through traffic. When I finally made it to the hospital, I had trouble getting the green knee scooter out of the car at first, but I was able to wiggle it out of the back seat after a few minutes of struggle. I almost lost my balance a slew of times as I traveled from my car, through the car garage, to the room Donna was in. I was relieved to see she was alive. She described the substantial damage her car sustained and how everything transpired.

After the medical staff finished running their tests and the police officer asked his questions about the accident, I was able to take her home. On the way home, we were advised to go to the tow truck company to acquire Donna's personal items from her totaled Nissan Rogue. The entire front end of the vehicle was completely demolished when we saw it. It was a miracle she was able to walk away from the accident physically unharmed, for the most part. As Donna was taking her possessions out of the vehicle, she couldn't help but become extremely emotional. We embraced and thanked God for sparing her life.

After a few weeks, I was finally able to move around without restrictions and return to work. Consequently, I had to deal with the embarrassment of rolling around campus on my knee scooter while wearing a walking boot. Thank God, my doctor cleared me after I made substantial improvements during my physical therapy sessions. The embarrassing aspect of it was the abundance of sympathy my students and the staff displayed upon my return. I've never been the type to be okay with anyone feeling sorry for me, so I'd usually refrain from sharing many of my personal struggles with others.

Going back to school in that condition was definitely difficult, but I had to set my pride aside and try to embrace the well-wishes and concern I'd receive from everyone. The rest of the school year went by decently as I healed and returned to some sense of normalcy.

New Season, New Hope (2019-2020)

The 2019-2020 basketball season was seen as our best chance to finally get over the hump and win the county championship. Everybody knew this year would be different from the years prior. To ensure we would be successful, I asked Coach Melissa to be my assistant. Ironically, the coach's daughter, a 6th grader, was also on our team, so it was only right for the coach to join me and add more invaluable coaching experience to our bench.

As an 8th grader, Netta knew the pressure was on; she knew she had to go out with a bang. I formulated a plan to capitalize on the influx of male athleticism on campus. I decided to create an all-male scout team to help with our practices. The idea paid immediate dividends because our team was battling every day against young men who were bigger, faster, and stronger than they were. As a result, when the time came to compete against other young ladies, they dominated. Everyone in the community would attend our home games to see the girls put on an offensive/defensive show. We outscored all our opponents, 400 to 55, within the first nine games of the regular season. Netta put on a masterclass by averaging 22.5 points per game.

I was so proud of the team as a whole because they displayed the type of killer instinct needed to eventually become champions. I knew we were going to finally get over the hump and win it all. Little did we know that we would never get a chance to finish the season and win the district title. Some of my colleagues and I were hearing rumors about adults and students getting sick throughout the state with some mysterious illness. Then abruptly, our perfect 9-0 season was cancelled, and in-person learning was discontinued for the foreseeable future. There were many devastating things that resulted from the transition from in-person learning to virtual learning. Some of those things consisted of the loss of friends and loved ones, not having the chance to say goodbye to my students, and the lack of social interaction everyone had to endure.

When COVID hit and shut everything down, everyone was devastated. Nicole didn't understand what was going on because she was only seven years old, and Netta was emotionally torn to shreds. The biggest issue with her was that she would miss out on many potential wonderful events that were associated with being an 8th grader. Since Donna worked in the healthcare industry, she unfortunately had to go to work as usual, relying only on the word of God, medical-grade masks, and latex gloves for protection.

To keep some sense of normalcy around the house, we'd do things like going into the garage or driveway to work out and watching tons of Netflix movies together. Other than that, it was tough to imagine the world never returning to normal. Everyone was on high alert due to the various news stations reporting that people were being hospitalized and many were even dying.

Kids everywhere had to continue school virtually. For me, teaching students remotely was a pain, especially without proper training on the Google Classroom platform. Most of my students paid attention and met my daily expectations, though a few took full advantage of not having to be in school physically. Some students played video games while logged into my Google Classroom, and others watched television. Occasionally, there were things students would display on their end that were quite concerning and grounds for virtual discipline referrals. It was all strange and unfamiliar territory, leading all teachers and administrators to use a lot of trial and error.

Even though there was a lot of uncertainty about the future of the free world, some things continued. One of those things that never stopped was travel basketball. We knew things would look different, but the show didn't stop. As long as college scouts and coaches agreed to continue recruiting players, there were always tournaments to attend, both far and near.

During these events, there were strict rules and guidelines all over the country. All spectators were screened for fevers with digital thermometers. Most people and even some of the players wore masks at all times, even during the games. It was weird and warranted due to the seriousness of the situation. It was tough to enforce social distancing because of the large number of people who attended the tournaments. Some people disregarded any safeguards that were put in place. As for my family and me, we mostly took all safety measures seriously. Surprisingly, Netta and her teammates played well, all things considered.

The travel arrangements to and from each tournament around the country were beyond terrifying. There were frequent delays at airports because each plane had to undergo thorough cleaning before anyone could board. At all checkpoints, before reaching the terminals, all passenger's temperatures were taken. While on the planes, nearly all passengers and flight attendants would wear face coverings. If someone sneezed or coughed, everyone would tense up and look around, feeling both disgusted and concerned. The majority of the people who continued to travel often during the pandemic were on high alert.

During the nationwide pandemic, Donna and I faced a tough decision about where to send Netta for high school the following year. One thing was for sure: the schools in Palm Beach weren't going to cut it, from an athletic perspective. Academically, we knew she wouldn't have an issue wherever she went because of how great she did throughout her time in elementary and middle school. She excelled in her advanced and high school credit courses while at Palm Springs. Due to the previous fiasco a year ago with Heritage, we figured the private schools in the area were out of the question as well.

Eventually, we started toying with the idea of possibly sending her out of the county to Blanche Ely High in Pompano Beach (which was where the director of her travel organization coached). Their basketball team won the state championship that year, and they had a slew of Division 1 prospects on their squad. Though the school had a less-than-desirable reputation due to its tumultuous neighborhood, we figured that type of environment could help prepare her for college and life in general. With all things considered, we also didn't have an idea of how long students would remain on the "distance learning" track.

The key obstacle in sending Netta to Ely was finding someone with an address we could use to enroll her there. We knew it wouldn't be ethical or legal, but we were reaching a point of desperation as we tried to find a suitable school for her to attend. We also found out it would only take a 20 to 25 minute car ride to get her from our house to Ely every day.

After some careful analysis, Donna and I pondered the potential ramifications of sending her to a school out of the county. We knew it could be an issue if anyone found out she was going to a school in another county, even though she was still residing in Palm Beach. We also knew there could be many disgruntled coaches from the Palm Beach area who might blow the whistle and file a report to the Florida High School Athletic Association. Instead of using deception and sneakiness, we decided to look for a new house in the Broward County area and put our current home on the market.

After a few months of searching, we finally found a wonderful 2-story house for which we would put in a competitive offer. Regarding our current home, we received a great offer and jumped at the chance to accept it. Before we knew it, during the peak of the pandemic, we were packing up and moving to the biggest home either of us had ever lived in. Thanks to our realtor's superb negotiating skills, we ended up with a few thousand dollars in our pocket, which we used to upgrade the house's interior before moving our furniture in. With this new residence, we would be able to apply for Netta to get into Ely's Magnet Program.

As far as our youngest daughter's school arrangements were concerned, we decided to keep her in the same elementary school she was attending in Palm Beach. The plan would be for me to drop her off at school on my way to work in the mornings and pick her up from the aftercare program when I get off work. Beyond the current school year, Nicole knew it would be her choice whether she would transfer to Broward County or not. Her mom and I thought she would like to stay at her current school until she finished elementary school, as she had made many friends at Coral Reef over the years. Thankfully, everything worked out, even though it looked bleak at one point.

A big part of moving back down to Broward was the ability to be closer to the rest of our families. Many things were happening among our families that warranted us to become more hands-on than we were before. My dad's health deteriorated severely. Visiting him in that state took a lot out of me. I would try to talk to him, but with the blank stare in his eyes and the sudden muscle spasms, I could tell there was no hope in expecting a response.

Every time I'd visit him, I felt like a piece of me was dying. I would always think about the what-ifs of our lives together. I figured if he didn't use drugs back in the day, he probably wouldn't have been in the shape he was in, until I found out his diseases were hereditary.

Recognition (2020)

At Palm Springs Middle, I developed many meaningful relationships with students, fellow teachers, and staff members over the past few years. I was considered one of the top teachers in the ELA department due to my ability to connect with all my students, regardless of who they were, and my ability to motivate them to excel academically and behaviorally.

Mrs. Jinks, the longtime principal there, was so impressed with my progress that she nominated me for the 2021 William T. Dwyer Award for Excellence in Education. Though I didn't make it as a finalist, I was still honored that my hard work was noticed and appreciated by my principal and colleagues.

Potential for Growth (2021)

One evening in September, I received a phone call from a friend from my old school. He said he was interested in going to another school because he wanted to grow professionally. He asked me about my plans, and I honestly didn't know how to answer, but he did spark a certain level of curiosity in me. I realized in my current position, I'd grown complacent due to my comfort level.

I decided to go online to our district website to look for vacant positions that were out there. Maybe something would catch my eye, maybe not. I spent about an hour combing through the listings until I spotted a resource teacher position with the Department of Safe Schools. The description of the role was very vague, so I went for it and applied to see what would happen. To my surprise, I received a call and was given a date and time for an interview. Also, during the phone call, I was told the position dealt with Classroom Management, amongst other things. Classroom Management was an area I specialized in during the bulk of my time as a teacher.

When I attended the interview, I did a great job. The panel seemed visibly impressed with all the responses to the questions I was asked. About a week or so later, I was offered the position. Though I wouldn't receive a pay increase, the notion of a flexible schedule and having the ability to work with struggling teachers was attractive. I would have the opportunity to give educators some of the tools and knowledge I'd acquired over the years.

The major catch to the job offer was convincing the newly appointed principal at my school to release me, as the new role would be considered a lateral move. When I approached her about the potential position, she told me she understood the opportunity, but she would be lying if she said she was thrilled with my leaving. She wanted me to give her a few weeks to find a replacement for me before I left, which I agreed to. Though we reached a tentative agreement, I could tell she didn't want to release me, since it was essentially the beginning of the year. After a few weeks, she found a replacement to take over my classes, and the next step was breaking the news to all of my students.

When I broke the news to my students, they understandably bombarded me with a litany of tough questions that I carefully answered. I didn't want to come off as insensitive, so I kept my responses short and sweet to avoid mistakenly triggering them. Some of them cried immediately, and others were just infuriated. I couldn't help but feel as if I was abandoning them.

For some reason, it felt like déjà vu from the time I left the previous school, a few years ago. Before I left, the principal sent out a school-wide email congratulating me on my new position within the district. I was showered with praise for a job well done while at Palm Springs, and the majority of them were sad to see me go. My last day was somber and surreal. I started second-guessing the hasty decision I made to leave. The last thing I ever wanted to do was let anyone down, especially my students.

Nevertheless, that was one of those times when I had to do what was best for me, professionally. The guilt of leaving started to eat at me. I believe my past issues with my mother skipping town on my father and me contributed to my attachment issues. All I kept thinking was, "Who knows, maybe things wouldn't work out at my new job and I'd end up back at Palm Springs one day."

The particulars of the new position were a lot to take in, at first. I was used to operating within the confines of my own classroom, essentially outside the public eye. The new job forced me to work on my marketability and sharpen my public speaking skills. While going through the training process, I noticed my new coworkers were extremely experienced, and they each had their own niches that made them ultra-engaging and relatable. I knew before long, I'd have to fine-tune my own style, especially if I wanted to be an impactful presenter. Our team was essentially responsible for the professional development training on classroom management throughout the entire district.

Granny (March 2022)

On March 7^{th,} our beloved Granny was called home to be with the Lord. It was beyond rough for all of us. She was eighty-one years old when she passed away, and all of us knew she lived her life to the fullest. The toughest thing to come to grips with was the realization that no one lives forever, regardless of who they are.

My cousin and I were asked to speak about our fondest memories of her during the funeral service. He went first, and then I followed up with a passionate yet emotional recollection of the great moments Granny and I shared. I also spoke about the importance of family sticking together, regardless of anyone's past transgressions, misunderstandings, or petty disagreements. At the moment, I briefly got choked up thinking about all the time that was lost.

After not speaking to my family due to the situation that occurred after Nicole was born, I was ashamed of the amount of distance I placed between myself and the people I loved. I missed birthdays, milestones, and holiday celebrations when all I had to do was set aside my pride and have those difficult conversations that needed to be had. The message I was delivering during Granny's funeral was basically a message to myself. Internally, I vowed to keep an open line of communication with my entire family, regardless of what happened in the past.

Enjoying Netta's Journey (2020-2024)

Academically, everyone knew there wouldn't be an issue for Netta in meeting the expected standard of excellence, no matter what high school she attended. On the contrary, when Netta started playing high school ball at Ely, her mother and I didn't know what to expect, considering the team was returning seven players from the prior year's championship run.

I'd hoped she'd do well enough in practice to earn substantial minutes off the bench, considering that her expertise was sharpshooting. A sharpshooter was basically a player who specializes in consistently making shots all over the court, mid-range, three-pointers, etc. Sharpshooters are known for having the ability to demoralize their opponents by hitting shots at a rate that most players couldn't dream of. It was a skill her team needed to replace because the three-point specialist from last year graduated.

Since Netta was now in high school, I wouldn't be as hands-on as years prior, but I would often meet her at the local park after practice. The purpose was to help her get extra shots up so she could further sharpen her consistency. I knew she had a tall task of trying to crack the starting lineup.

To our surprise, her name was among those called for the starting lineup right before tip-off of the first game of the regular season. She definitely didn't play like a freshman either. By scoring 16 points and making 4 3-pointers, she let it be known she was ready for all the smoke. From that game forward, it was clear to see that Netta was an important piece to another championship-caliber team. By the season's end, she earned second-team all-county honors, and she had made a name for herself in Broward County. The next three years would be a wild ride, filled with thrilling game-winning shots, heated rivalries, and tons of excitement for the family. Every season, I'd create highlight videos and send them out to every Division 1 and Division 2 coaching staff in the country who had social media accounts. My thought process was a little different from most parents when it came to the recruiting process. Many parents felt it was the responsibility of high school and travel coaches to get their players recruited by college coaches; my philosophy was that it's the responsibility of the parents, coaches, and players collectively.

My due diligence in bringing her videos to the public's attention paid off, and I was able to help Netta have a few meaningful conversations with the coaching staff at Bethune-Cookman University in Daytona Beach. These conversations led to a scholarship offer and an eventual commitment. I was just proud I was able to help her in achieving one of her goals, which was earning a full scholarship to college.

Rest in Peace (2024)

After the new year, my dad was rushed to the hospital because he was having a hard time breathing due to already having a PEG Tube in his belly for feeding purposes. They also inserted a catheter for urinating, and that, along with everything else, made it apparent his quality of life was less than ideal.

The doctor informed my sister and I of our possible options for him, and we made the tough decision to allow for his transfer to hospice care. I knew if my dad were mentally and physically well, he wouldn't want to stick around while hooked up to wires, tubes, and machines for the rest of his time on this earth. Besides, the medical staff let us know he would be able to pass away peacefully instead of in pain and agony. Upon his transfer, we all took turns sitting with him during the day and in the evenings. I remember whispering in his ear, telling him my sister and I were good, and that it was fine to go ahead and get his rest. A part of me felt he was hanging on for us. He probably just wanted to know his kids were going to be alright before he passed away.

On January 12, a couple of hours after I left the medical center, a nurse called to inform me that my dad had died. After hanging up the phone, my entire body went numb. My dad was gone forever! The only person on this earth who really knew me. The one with whom I went through so many trials and tribulations. Truth be told, I wanted to go with him, and if it wasn't for my wife, kids, and my love for God, I would've probably done something drastic to be with him.

***

One of the good things about my family members was that when business needed to be taken care of, someone always stepped up to the plate to get things done. As far as the home-going celebration was concerned, I told my Aunt Teresa, Aunt Erica, Uncle Stetson, and my sister that my dad wouldn't want a sad traditional funeral, nor did he want to be buried. I remembered years ago when he was of sound mind and body, my dad stated he wanted certain songs from his favorite artist, Tupac Shakur, played throughout the celebration. He also told me that if anyone showed up whom he didn't like, he would personally throw them out, by all means necessary.

Remembering the type of dude my dad was, he was earnest when he made the statement, so I kept it in the back of my mind. When I initially told my aunts and uncles what he would've wanted and how he would've wanted it, one of them disagreed at first. Thankfully, with a little persuasion, they came around. The rest of our family and I respected his wishes, and instead of having an old-fashioned funeral in a church, we had a memorial celebration at a banquet hall. Surprisingly, I was able to keep my emotions intact until we all started reminiscing about my dad, and I broke down in tears for a few minutes. I had to walk outside to regain my composure.

Looking at his picture and realizing I would never see him again in his physical form caused unbearable pain for me. It was the type of pain that I was unable to fathom until that exact moment. From that day on, I'd dedicate the rest of my life to carrying on his legacy and making him proud.

www.ingramcontent.com/pod-product-compliance
Lightning Source LLC
Chambersburg PA
CBHW030908120626
46554CB00001B/63